D0221346

Nashville
Public Library
Foundation

*This book
made possible
through generous gifts
to the
Nashville Public Library
Foundation Book Fund*

lessons
to learn

lessons
to learn

voices from the front lines of
teach for america

molly ness

RoutledgeFalmer
Taylor & Francis Group

NEW YORK AND LONDON

Published in 2004 by
RoutledgeFalmer
29 West 35th Street
New York, NY 10001
www.routledge-ny.com

Published in Great Britain by
RoutledgeFalmer
11 New Fetter Lane
London EC4P 4EE
www.routledgefalmer.com

RoutledgeFalmer is an imprint of the Taylor & Francis Group.

Printed in the United States of America on acid-free paper.

Library of Congress Cataloging-in-Publication Data available.

ISBN 0-415-945909 (hardcover: alk. paper)

To Mom and Dad, with love and gratitude

Out of poverty comes poetry,
Out of despair, music.

—**Mexican proverb**

contents

acknowledgments

This book was a community effort. It is impossible to write a book comprised of well over a hundred interviews without being eternally grateful to those who assisted in the endeavor.

First and foremost, Ted Weinstein, the best agent around, was an absolute delight. His responsiveness, intelligence, and high standards made me work harder and better. His tireless work on my behalf has never gone unnoticed.

Many thanks to the good people of Routledge for their belief in this project and for their wise thoughts and guidance.

I hardly know where to begin in thanking the interviewees, for their time, energy, and their eager participation. The members of the Teach For America community spoke with candor, thoughtfulness, and passion about their experiences. Their creative and diligent work as teachers and social advocates inspired me to keep working, even on the days when writing felt like a chore. I appreciate the particular corps members and alums who extended themselves to me time and time again— through writing, multiple phone calls, e-mail exchanges, and editorial assistance. Let me extend my apologies to the interviewees for whom I glossed over the complexity of their work. This was done solely because of time limits and page restraints and does not accurately reflect the importance of their experiences. I would also like to thank the participants outside of Teach For America, including principals, superintendents, parents, professors, and researchers. They provide valuable voices in the ongoing debates surrounding public education.

Certain members of the Teach For America National Office deserve a sincere thanks. Melissa Golden was always willing to answer questions, send along information, and back this project. The Teach For America regional staffs were incredibly kind in providing me with contact names and information, and taking me to tour schools to see corps members in action. Wendy Kopp has inspired so much of this entire experience, not only my writing, but my work as a corps member.

A solid cadre of wonderful, wonderful, and even more wonderful friends has supported me in the book and beyond. A million thanks go to Rob Hunt for his constant cheerleading, his unending patience, and for simply being the best friend I could ever ask for. Anthony Mato, Blake McCallister, Katherine Onorato, Ariel Pepple, Charlotte Riggs, Andy Snow, and Duane Wheatcroft are fantastic beyond words. My friends and colleagues at the Curry School of Education have been impeccable advocates and educators. Mary Abouzeid, Suzanne Boone, Suzanne Esterson, Ana Hummel, Jody Kahn, Susan Mintz, Jessica Ramsey, and Maggie Reed deserve my most earnest thanks. David Portnoy is a teacher and mentor extraordinaire. Jay Carney was kind enough to read the earliest draft of this book and then walk with me in its progression.

My sixth graders at Roosevelt Middle School in Oakland, California, are a source of inspiration in writing and life. They exemplify courage, grace, and resiliency. They never gave up on me, and I, in turn, never gave up on them. Wherever they are in life, I remain their biggest advocate and admirer.

My family has given me undying support and unconditional love. How can I even begin to thank the people who gave me the roots for my foundation and the wings for my future?

author's note

In 1998, the Department of Education released sobering statistics. Nearly 70 percent of inner-city and rural fourth graders cannot read at even a basic level. Children growing up in low-income communities are seven times less likely to graduate from college than those in high-income areas. Our nation's public schools are plagued by an achievement gap, a inequity in academic performance between poor children and rich children. In 1989, Wendy Kopp, a Princeton senior, was nagged by this inequity and envisioned a solution: The nation's most outstanding recent college graduates would put their degrees to work by teaching in low-income communities. The result was Teach For America, the national corps of recent college graduates who commit two years to teach in the county's neediest urban and rural public schools. In the thirteen years since its creation, Teach For America has selected a yearly corps of highly competitive college graduates, trained them during a summer institute, placed them as full-time, paid teachers in under-resourced schools, and coordinated a support network to help them succeed in their two years of teaching.

Teach For America attracts college graduates who develop ambitious visions for social change, who are passionate about ensuring that all children in the nation will have an equal chance in life, and who work relentlessly to overcome obstacles. They are bright and enthusiastic, as well as flexible and adaptable; a Teach For America corps member must be prepared for a history placement and then teach math. The two-year Teach For America commitment is a journey that often begins with idealism and progresses to disillusionment as the realities of public education set in. The Teach For America experience is not over after two years; the organization looks to alumni as a leadership force with the insight and commitment to effect systemic change in law, policy, health, business, education, and many other arenas.

In 1999, I became a Teach For America corps member and spent the next two years teaching in Oakland, California. I didn't join because of my interest in teaching as a career, but because of my fervor for social equity. In my senior year, I read Jonathan Kozol's *Savage Inequalities*, which opened my eyes to the bleak world of public schooling in inner-city communities. Students—in the most prosperous country in the world—attended schools where ceiling tiles crumbled on their heads, where they read outdated textbooks. And the crisis did not end at schools. Poverty, for children in low-income areas, meant lack of access to quality housing, to health care and nutrition, and greater exposure to drug use and violence. The book stirred a new sense of outrage in me, as well as a sense of my own sheltered life. I grew up in a world of prep school uniforms, where students chose classes like Advanced Placement French Literature and U.S. History Since 1945, and where science labs were stocked with brand-new microscopes and dissection kits. My own societal contributions and improvement were too minimal and too sporadic. I didn't want to be a person who pointed to the problems and said, "When is someone going to do something about that?" I wanted to roll up my sleeves and get my hands messy in the process of making the world a bit better than the way I found it.

At the time, the 1999 corps of 768 members was the largest corps yet, with college grades, SAT scores, and leadership ranked at an all-time high. As a rookie teacher, I was assigned to teach sixth grade Social Studies and English in Oakland, California. The challenge was immediate and overwhelming. The school, originally built to house seven hundred students, served 1,200 Asian, African-American, and Latino students. On an average day, nearly one hundred students came through my classroom doors. I taught written and conversational English to students whose native languages were Arabic, Cantonese, Cambodian, Bosnian, Vietnamese, Korean, Mien, and Spanish. Some were recent immigrants who had fled war-torn countries. Others grew up in the United States, but spoke their native languages at home.

Like any first-year teacher, I struggled both personally and professionally. I quickly realized that I was, by no means, adequately prepared for the classroom. I wondered if I was doing my students a huge disservice. I questioned my presence in a community where my skin color and my background made me feel like an outsider. I even felt disappointed by the lack of guidance and mentoring that Teach For America provided. I felt too often it was taboo as a Teach For America corps member to feel frustrated by the obstacles that added to the challenge of teaching: under-resourced schools, bureaucratic headaches, disengaged students and families. Yet I took consolation in knowing that I was a part of a nationwide movement to give students who lived and learned in poverty an equal chance in life. I had joined thousands of other past and present corps members who fought similar battles, in Compton, along the banks of the Mississippi Delta, and in the dusty classrooms of South Texas. I knew I was not the sole voice of skepticism about teaching and about Teach For America; my fellow corps members surely wondered if they were cut out for this line of work and even toyed with the idea of leaving. I may have been alone in my tiny classroom, but I was a part of something much larger: a national support network, a community effort, a grassroots organization that demanded social justice and educational reform. That esprit de corps carried me through my integration into a community with a rich history and diversity, through learning from and working alongside veteran teachers, and witnessing growth and improvement in schools, districts, and states. Teach For America was an incredibly challenging and unbelievably rewarding experience.

In my first two years with Teach For America, and the years since, I have been intrigued by the thousands of stories of success, of struggle, and of perseverance that have arisen from corps members. I have written this book to tell their stories of hope and determination, and portray Teach For America as merely one step in public school reform. I believe that Teach For America is not a solution to the problems in public education, but the net pros of the program outweigh its cons. I must clarify that this book represents my take on Teach For America. The following is my best effort to give a comprehensive overview of the Teach For America experience and a critical examination of its impact. It is my hope that one day our nation will see a day when teaching is a legitimate, financially sound profession and that urban and rural schools will not have to rely on Teach For America to fill their teaching vacancies. Until our public policy and education funding make this vision a possibility, programs like Teach For America, which funnel ill-prepared, uncertified teachers into the neediest schools will continue to exist.

This book was written over the course of six months, during which I conducted 154 interviews with Teach For America corps members, staff, and alumni, as well as people from outside the corps—education professors, researchers, reporters, parents, students, principals, and superintendents. Within the corps, I spoke to members from all regions, years, and placements. I spoke with alumni who remain in the field of education, and those who left to pursue very different careers. I found my interviewees through a variety of methods. Some I knew personally from my own time as a corps member. Others I received through the Teach For America alumni network, its computer databank, and its biannual alumni newsletter. In many cases, I pounded the pavement to find participants. I read articles about people and their achievements. I asked the Teach For America national and regional staffs as well as corps members themselves to assist me. I hounded people through e-mail and phone calls. The response was overwhelming; I was flooded with responses from eager participants. Corps members and alumni were kind enough to speak with me candidly, to open up their classroom doors to me, and to send me their own speeches, journal entries, and other written reflections. Interviews lasted typically from thirty minutes to an hour, and all participants fact-checked their own write-ups for accuracy. I have done my best to give accurate reflections of interviews. Participation was entirely voluntary, permissions were obtained, and nearly all participants agreed to attach their names with their quotes and experiences. Five corps members' names have been changed to protect privacy at their request. Pseudonyms were given to students and schools.

To the best of my ability, I tried to represent the Teach For America corps as evenly as I could, keeping in mind that race, gender, and socioeconomic background may shape a corps member's feelings about their classroom experience. In addition, I attempted to be evenhanded in my interviews—inviting corps members who responded "I'm not a Teach For America cheerleader" to voice their own concerns and critiques. The voices of critical inquiry, after all, will push Teach For America along its continued path of self-reflection, constant learning, and future improvement.

Even with my conscious efforts to be evenhanded, the dilemma remains that Teach For America is a complex and loaded issue. Writing about our nation's schools is a delicate subject; it is nearly impossible to reflect the state of public education without touching on politics, socioeconomic factors, race, ethnicity, not to mention the larger debates over teacher training and educational reform. In presenting the challenges and realities of urban and rural schools, I grappled with how much to tell, with what to tell, and with the reasons of why to tell. The portrayal of our schools is not always flattering. Let me be clear here: I write about schools with overcrowded classrooms, poor resources, and urban strife simply to represent the realities. I do not intend to attach judgment to the schools, the communities, or their staffs, students, or leadership. In fact, my experience as a 1999 Oakland corps member was that students reached great accomplishments in the face of adversity, that teachers and school leaders engaged in reflective dialogue and creative solutions, and that parents and communities collaborated to translate educational equity into reality. I write about the realities as a means to carry out the second part of Teach For America's mission of effecting change through different venues. I see myself using words to increase readers' sense of urgency that our schools need significant reform through funding, increased support, and innovative ideas. That being said, let's envision a day in which students are not stunted by these realities, but are constantly engaged, motivated, and invested in public education.

Additionally, I write about the successes of Teach For America corps members not to imply that they are saviors in a public education crisis, but to show that young people with little training in difficult circumstances can make significant classroom contributions. Teach For America corps members are not immune to the challenges, stumbling blocks, and failures that are inherent in being a rookie teacher. Many schools, communities, and fellow educators attach a sense of elitism to Teach For America and its corps members. After all, the majority of corps members are young, white, educated, and come from upper-middle-class backgrounds. I can't help but think of the words of a fellow teacher at my school, a teacher of thirty years who had grown up in the community where she taught. She stated, "These young white folks sweep into our communities with no real understanding of our people, our problems, and what will constitute our solutions." In an effort to be sensitive to how they are perceived, many corps members enter their classrooms without advertising their affiliation with Teach For America. Moreover, the success of corps members and the organization as a whole simply wouldn't be possible without the graciousness, guidance, and support of veteran teachers, school districts, and administrators. I hope future corps members will carry this understanding and this humility into their own classrooms.

It is difficult to capture the precise essence of Teach For America, since it is an organization that is constantly evolving. In a million different ways, Teach For America has matured, refocused, and transformed. What began as an organization to fill classroom vacancies has re-created itself to narrow the achievement gap. The Teach For America of 1994 was very different than the Teach For America that I knew in 1999. Likewise, the Teach For America of today will be far different than one five or ten years down the road. With that in mind, much of what I write about professional development, training, and recruitment are already said and done, and have already been reflected upon and changed for the future.

As the TFA alumni network nears ten thousand, it is impossible to include enough voices to create the comprehensive oral history of Teach For America. There are just too many stories to tell. Throughout the writing process, I had an insatiable desire to interview more people. My first goal was to interview fifty participants. That soon changed to one hundred, and even then I felt the need to raise that bar. My book is a starting point for the thousands of stories. I encourage every Teach For America corps member, past and present, to tell his or her own stories. Telling the stories is perhaps one of the best ways these young teachers can continue to be advocates for the students who taught them life lessons, the families who shared their lives, and the communities that welcomed them.

chapter one

the birth of a vision

I hope young Americans all across the country think about joining Teach For America. There is no better way to leave a mark, a positive mark on the life of America.
　　　　　—President George W. Bush announces his plan to expand national service at Booker T. Washington High School in Atlanta, Georgia, January 31, 2002.

The morning bell rings at Walker Elementary in Washington, D.C.'s, northwest corner. Five hundred students stampede through the hallways, slam locker doors shut, and scurry off to classrooms. A line of fifth grade students forms outside of Room 202, where teacher Brian La Macchia stands at the door. Brian is white and he is young. He has no previous classroom experience and his Teach For America placement is his first real job. Twenty students push and shove in line until they stand on the threshold of the door, where Brian La Macchia greets every student with a friendly "Good morning, Celeste" and "Nice to see you, Omar." The students, clad in yellow and maroon uniforms, file to their seats as sunlight trickles through windows covered in crisscross metal bars.

Brian takes his place in the front of the room and bellows out "Good morning, everyone." The still groggy class responds with a meek, "Good morning, Mr. La Macchia." Brian glances up from the stack of papers with a look of disappointment. "That was weak. Let's do that again." And with this extra prompting, the class responds with an enthusiastic, sing-song "Good morning, Mr. La Macchia." Class is in session. Brian begins, "Can someone tell me what we did last time in class?" Hands shoot up. A small African-American girl, hair in corn-rows, is chosen and she confidently recounts the details from the last class. She stumbles once, and Brian assists her with an encouraging, "You got it."

After a quick review, the moment the students have been waiting for arrives. Brian instructs, "I'll let you get started on your labs now." There are shouts of joy, exclamations of "Yes!" and almost entirely inde-pendently, students find their lab groups and set to work. They use yardsticks to measure off three hundred centimeters, put masking tape on the floor to mark their positions, and move chairs to each end of the tape marks. They string fishing line between the two chairs and dangle airplanes fashioned out of popsicle sticks and drinking straws from the fishing line. They take turns cranking plastic propellers, which are wound by rubber bands, and cheer as their planes zip from chair to chair. The classroom is abuzz in activity, students cheering on class-mates, testing and retesting their scientific hypotheses, and conversing with Mr. La Macchia about their discoveries. When students are asked how they feel about their teacher, they report, "I learn a lot from him," "It's fun in there," and "He took us to the city chess tournament. We almost won the championship. We had timers and everything."

The spirit and enthusiasm for learning in this classroom is conta-gious. These students—all African Americans and Latinos, nearly all qualifying for free or reduced lunches—are precisely the type of stu-dents who usually are stunted by the realities of the achievement gap. But in this room, there are no excuses to prevent learning, not the poverty or the backgrounds of the students, not the young age and inexperience of the teacher.

Along the hills of northeastern North Carolina, twenty-four-year-old Tia Lendo wakes up and drives to Parker Street Elementary School. She too is young and white. Tia came to Teach For America upon graduating from the University of North Carolina, looking to extend the community service efforts she made in college. At first glance, she may appear to be an outsider in the community—one of the few white Northerners in an area where racial segregation has deep roots. Her fourth grade classroom is composed of seventeen African-American students, who have grown up surrounded by intense rural poverty. All but one of her students qualify for free or reduced school lunches. Even in the fourth grade, her students come to school at a variety of levels. Some are reading at the first grade level, whereas others are on grade level. Some struggle to sound out words; others have never read a chapter book by themselves.

Tia, however, never looks at these realities and sees them as a crutch. She constantly pushes them to love reading and to become critical thinkers. On this November morning, the students complete pre-reading activities for their new chapter book. They are about to begin Louis Sachar's *Holes*, which is written at a fifth grade reading level, though neighboring schools are teaching the same book to their sixth and ninth grade students. Tia's fourth graders analyze the book cover, make predictions about the story's course of events, and hypothesize about the book's issues of concern. Tia coaches them through conversations like, "What are some characteristics of good readers?" These fourth graders toss around words like "theme," "characterization," and "protagonist" with ease. By the end of the year, this is a classroom of readers, who add *The Giver*, *James and the Giant Peach*, and *Charlotte's Web* to the list of the books they've finished. And Tia's work extends after school hours and outside school walls. On a Saturday morning, Tia's students, most of whom had not been beyond their rural town, load a school bus for a four-hour drive to the beach towns of North Carolina's Outer Banks. They study the science of tidal ecosystems, visit the sites where the Wright Brothers flew the first airplanes, and return home exhausted but invigorated.

Before she arrived in North Carolina, 39% of Tia's students passed the state end-of-grade test in reading. After two years of teaching, 59% passed. Her goal as a third-year teacher is for 100% of her students to pass the end-of-grade-level tests in reading and math, to teach her students to become science and social studies scholars, to create a community of learners, and to have her students advance two grades in reading.

These accounts are not fictional, nor are they unusual for Teach For America. Brian La Macchia (1998, Washington, D.C.) and Tia Lendo (2000, North Carolina) are barely out of college. They have been placed in difficult schools in impoverished areas. Neither Brian nor Tia came to the classroom as a certified teacher. They did not major in education in college and they have never taught before. These teachers have little tangible support and little on-site job training, no one to hold their hands as they struggle through the challenges of their first year of teaching. Their schools face teacher turnover and rock-bottom state standardized test scores. They teach with minimal resources. Their classrooms are overcrowded. Almost 100% of their students are people of color and most have grown up in poverty. Ray Owens (1991, Los Angeles) described similar realities in the South Central Los Angeles school where he taught:

> The facility and the supplies were inadequate. I had never before been to a school that didn't have a library. I couldn't believe how overcrowded it was. In my first grade classroom, I had thirty-three students. Sometimes we didn't have enough desks. We spent the first months of school without textbooks. Right away it seemed that the conditions of the school set these students up for failure.

In Tunica, Mississippi—the third poorest county at the time—Cindy Zmijewski-Demers (1993, Mississippi) found that rural poverty translated into similar circumstances:

> My school, housing eleven hundred, virtually all of whom were African-American students, was totally run down. The bathrooms lacked the

basics of soap and tissue. An open sewer ran outside the school. Paint chips flaked off the walls. There weren't enough desks or textbooks for my biggest class of thirty-five. There were no pencils, no paper. In a town where the temperatures regularly reached over one hundred degrees, there was no air-conditioning.

It seems logical to assume that these teachers were destined for failure in their first years in the classroom. Yet, in spite of the odds being stacked against them, they rose to the challenge and persevered in the face of adversity. They did not merely do their jobs. They did much more than simply show up to school each day, slide worksheets under their students' noses, or teach out of workbooks. Many of these teachers achieved extraordinary success both in and out of the classroom. They start after-school tutoring clubs. They teach their eighth grade math students how to incorporate the basic math of graphs and charts into reading the rise and fall of the stock market. They write grants to buy computers for their classrooms. They take their students on camping trips, they coach football teams, and they encourage their students to go to college. These young, inexperienced Teach For America corps members have come to the classroom with aspirations to have a direct influence on academic achievement and with the belief that effective teaching is effective leadership.

Teach For America was founded on the vision that one day every child in the nation will have an opportunity to attain an excellent education. The organization's basic tenet is the dedication to the relentless pursuit for educational equity for students of low-income neighborhoods. Founded in 1989, Teach For America is the brainchild of Wendy Kopp, who proposed a national teacher corps as her senior thesis project at Princeton University. The idea of placing the best and brightest college graduates in the nation's poorest schools was equated with a domestic version of the Peace Corps. Kopp's vision took off slowly, with grants and philanthropic donations trickling in. Early contributors included Ross Perot, the Mobil Corporation, and Morgan Stanley. In its first year, 2,500 college graduates from one hundred colleges and universities responded to recruitment efforts. Five hundred corps members were selected to form the 1990 charter corps of Teach For America. Before being placed in six regions nationwide, the corps came together for an eight-week summer training institute lead by veteran teachers and teacher educators. In June 1994, Teach For America received a $2 million operating grant from the Corporation for National Service. As it exists today, Teach For America falls under the Americorps umbrella, the national public service network.

Teach For America is no stranger to the media spotlight. Over the years, it has received a tremendous amount of media attention, including coverage in *USA Today, The New York Times,* and *The Washington Times.* President Wendy Kopp has been interviewed by a myriad of sources, including National Public Radio, *Good Morning America,* and *NewsHour with Jim Lehrer.* First Lady Laura Bush spent a week in 2001 touring Teach For America classrooms in Washington, D.C. Members of the United States House of Representatives listened to Jonathan Brenner (1996, New York) testify that applying to Teach For America was "the best decision of my life." Teach For America literally has lived its organizational history under public scrutiny.

Some of the media attention is brought on by the organization itself, through the 1997 creation of Teach For America Week, an annual nationwide event in which leaders from all professions spend an hour as guest teachers in Teach For America classrooms. The list of invitees includes politicians, business leaders, athletes, performers, and community activists, including actor Noah Wylie, Ronnie Lott of the San Francisco 49ers, Lynne Cheney, wife of Vice President Dick Cheney, Oprah Winfrey, Surgeon General D. David Satcher, political strategist James Carville, Attorney General Janet Reno, actor Arnold Schwarzenegger, Henry Kissinger, and Olympic medalist Dan Jansen. Guest teachers engage students, encourage them to continue in school, and share knowledge and words of wisdom.

Since its inception, Teach For America has strengthened its foundation, solidified its mission, and become highly selective in recruitment and selection. The organization has grown tremendously in size, has responded to public criticism, has floundered with economic hardships, and has nearly collapsed. In 1994, start-up funds dried up and Teach For America was nearly $1.2 million in debt. A *Phi Delta Kappan* article called Teach For America "bad policy and bad education." With this negative press, donors shied away. Since then, Teach For America has been rebuilt to place over ten thousand talented and committed individuals in classrooms. Today, corps members serve in twenty of the nation's most impoverished school districts: in urban areas such as Baltimore, Los Angeles, Chicago, and New York and in rural areas such as the Rio Grande Valley and the Mississippi Delta. In the first thirteen years, Teach For America corps members have taught over 1.25 million students nationwide. Since 1990, Teach For America has received over 65,000 applications. In an average year, approximately one thousand corps members are chosen from nearly four thousand to five thousand applicants, with an acceptance rate hovering between 20–25%. For the 2003 corps, Teach For America received nearly 16,000 applications.

Over the years, support has trickled in from the principals and superintendents of schools where corps members are placed. In August 2001, Teach For America conducted a survey to measure principals' satisfaction with corps members' classroom performance. In telephone interviews and questionnaires from 322 principals, Teach For America yielded the following results:

> Principals are pleased to have Teach For America corps members in their schools. They credit these teachers as being highly motivated, energetic, enthusiastic, and committed to children and to teaching. Corps members are seen as intelligent, creative, highly educated, and knowledgeable about their subjects.

The following statistics are results from the study:

- 77% of principals rate corps members as above average compared to other beginning teachers.

- 97% of principals rate corps members as advantageous for the school and its students.

Principal Paul Johnson is one of the Teach For America's advocates. In fall 2002, six corps members taught at his Newark K–8 school. In discussing the effectiveness of his corps members, Mr. Johnson cited that "some have moved to the top of the heap with regards to leadership desire and ability."

> There are some excellent educators already at a young age. If I come into a classroom, I expect to see kids engaged and motivated in learning. That is the sign of a teacher who is doing his job. Outcomes in terms of measurable data are all well and good, but they are abstract from my vantage point. I look to see well-embellished classrooms that foster learning. I look to these corps members with the responsibility of engaging their students to be on task. Teach For America is a wonderful part of the nation's curriculum and I applaud young people who are willing to share their gifts.

Above and beyond principals, support for Teach For America comes from district superintendents, like Carl Harris of Franklin County schools in rural North Carolina. Since 1994, approximately twelve to fifteen corps members have been placed in Franklin County schools each year. Harris's support for Teach For America comes from the dedication of corps members:

> They are highly committed to making a difference in the life of a child. Corps members recognize that they haven't come to the classroom through a traditional program and they consistently work at things to improve upon the areas where they aren't as proficient. They set high expectations for themselves. They support kids with additional time after school in academic and extracurricular settings. They are well prepared. They do a great job delivering instruction from multiple instruction levels to meet the needs of all children.

Harris credits Teach For America with selecting top-notch candidates:

> Their screening process is highly accurate in choosing people with
> adaptable personalities and good communication skills. These are peo-
> ple who have demonstrated their competency in academics. They bring
> an unwaivering commitment to make differences in the education of
> our young people, and they don't allow excuses to muddy that commit-
> ment. I am always asking for additional corps members.

This is not to say that Teach For America is without its flaws. In a 1996
Education Week article, Dennis Evans called Teach For America an "ill-
conceived and disastrous fiasco." Critics say that the five weeks of
training before going into some of the toughest classrooms is not sufficient, and that allowing underprepared teachers into the classroom
diminishes the standards for teaching. In the University of Virginia's
Cavalier Daily, Professor Susan Mintz of the Curry School of
Education wrote the following:

> America needs teachers, not Teach For America. In order to make a
> lasting difference on a child or in the classroom, teachers need system-
> atic opportunities to learn their profession and to perfect their craft.
> There are skills that TFA simply does not have the resources to provide
> in either breadth or depth.

Even veteran teachers may look warily at Teach For America; in a
2003 *Washington Post Magazine* interview, a veteran teacher at a
Washington, D.C., elementary school had this to say about corps
members:

> There's so much resentment about having them come into the schools.
> People would say the same things about the Teach For America kids
> that they used to say about us: "They need to go back where they came
> from, they need to stick to their own."

There is even skepticism from within the corps; Scrapha Reed (1995, New York) questions the motivation of the average TFAers:

> There are two general personality groups I have come across in Teach For America. There are the people who have a sincere interest to give back to their community and to develop the most prized members of the community, the hope of the future, the youth. Then there are others who have more self-serving motivations, even while thinking their motivations are altruistic in nature. They want to be involved in a project that distinguiches them from their peers, that allows them to go home on Thanksgiving break and tell their extended families how rough it is working in the school and neighborhoods they've been placed in, how hard it is to reach and teach the children, and basically how wonderful they are for passing up other opportunities to go and work with the less privileged. While I think the first group has made incredible contributions to the education and lives of many youth, the second group, sadly, is much greater in number.

Criticism also arises with regard to the recruitment policies; skeptics say that not enough is being done to recruit candidates from diverse cultural, socioeconomic, and racial backgrounds. Others wonder about how truthful Teach For America is in its recruitment efforts. Meghan Corman (2002, Los Angeles) explained, "TFA keeps a bit of the truth out of the public eye when they recruit. The corporate aspect feels a bit like propaganda." There are corps members who believe that Teach For America did not give them the tools to be successful teachers. William Jacobs (2001, New Mexico) learned to survive as a first-year teacher entirely independent of Teach For America:

> The leadership of my corps was unsupportive. I felt like Teach For America merely brought me to my placement and then dropped me. I didn't get anything from them, and I felt let down. I learned to make it through long hours, hard work, and outside research on effective teaching. In my first year, I definitely did not consider myself a Teach For

America corps member.

In the 1990 charter corps of 489, only 342, or 70%, fulfilled their two-year commitment. Over a decade later, the attrition rate remains a legitimate problem. Corps member Jay Carney (1999, Southern Louisiana) was one of the estimated 15% of corps members who did not complete their two-year commitment. Jay dropped out in the first month of teaching, and later came to believe that "Teach For America put me in a classroom where I could not succeed. The organization encourages intense two-year periods, not lifelong vocations." He questioned whether corps members can live up to Teach For America's high standards of excellence and accomplishment for long. "For my first month of teaching, I met with my students every night until 8 pm. If I had stayed in the classroom, would that have been true for the long haul?" Furthermore, Jay came to see Teach For America as a stopgap measure:

> People do a lot of good in two years, but almost immediately I noticed this undercurrent of negativity of the corps. It was sad. People had become what they said they wouldn't—cynical about Teach For America, feeling that they were merely trying to survive in the classroom. I felt that negativity happening to me, and I really didn't want that. I wanted to make a lifetime out of teaching and I felt if I stayed with Teach For America, I would forever turn away from teaching.

Critics look to the approximate 40% of corps members who finish their commitments and leave teaching for the private sector as proof that applicants view Teach For America as a stepping stone and a resumé builder, often contributing to the teacher turnover that plagues troubled schools. Steve Richards (2000, Baltimore) readily admitted that he came to Teach For America as a break before applying to law school. He had no intention of remaining in teaching or becoming "a permanent fixture in social justice or community issues." He believes that Teach For America causes misunderstandings with corps members, schools, and districts in presenting its image:

Teach For America presents itself one way when they recruit. They say this is a two-year Americorps program. After you get into the thick of things, they beat their drums about continuing the commitment, about how corps members need to become permanent fixtures in communities and the lives of students. I think a lot of people do have the mindset of bringing about long-term change, but perhaps those people are turned off by people like me who are in this for two years. Teach For America can be successful if they are merely looking to fill the void of teacher vacancies, but if they really want people to make long-term commitments, then they need to repackage themselves as a long-term deal. It is this misunderstanding and this gray area that causes a backlash. I was always honest about my intent to leave after two years. Teach For America needs to ask themselves, Is it logical to think that the top college grads will commit long-term to teaching in high-need areas?

Steve explained that his involvement in the mission of long-term change will be limited to reading relevant articles and voting in correspondence with issues. Yet he concluded, "As far as me pursuing an inner-city teaching career, it's not going to happen. This is not something I'll devote myself to."

Lessons to Learn: Voices from the Front Lines of Teach for America looks at the entire Teach For America journey—making the commitment and joining the corps, the challenges, realities, and successes of classroom placement, reflecting on the experience, and leaving the classroom as a profoundly different individual. The testimonials trace corps members through the emotional cycle of a first-year teacher: anticipation, survival, dissatisfaction, rejuvenation, and reflection. There are lessons to learn from these teachers, beyond the lessons of perseverance and determination. There are lessons about innovative ways to teach, about the obstacles that impede student learning, and about the reform that our schools so desperately need.

chapter two

making the commitment

On a rainy weekday night in Charlottesville, Virginia, fifty University of Virginia undergrads gather in a lecture hall. They trek across campus in the rain, turning down Thursday night invitations to parties or off-campus bars. They follow flyers reading "You want to change things." And though University of Virginia is home to one of the nation's top schools for teacher preparation, these undergrads have come for information on joining the non-traditional route into the classroom through Teach For America.

The room buzzes as the audience fills out contact cards, flips through glossy brochures, and gossips with neighbors. Dressed in a suit and tie, Scot Fishman (1997, Washington, D.C.) hardly looks the role of a former teacher. He stands to address the group and starts with an introduction. He left three years of teaching to become a University of Virginia law student and was hired by Teach For America as an on-campus recruiter.

"Let me start with a story about my fifth grader Donte," Scot begins his sales pitch. At once, the room is silent. "Donte was new to the school. He was so quiet that he'd walk up to me, tap me on the shoulder, and whisper to ask if he could go to the bathroom. In fourth grade, Donte had gotten low grades and was always pegged as being the root of classroom altercations." Almost subconsciously, Scot slips back into his teacher persona. He paces across the room, climbing the steps in the lecture hall. All eyes are on him, the audience engaged by his presence and his words. "Donte had high skills in math and reading. But these skills hadn't yet been tapped. He came to my classroom scoring below average on standardized tests." Scot pauses. "By the end of the year, Donte scored above basic in all reading and math parts of that same test."

Scot hesitates again, allowing his story to sink in. He returns to the Teach For America script on how to lead campus information sessions, in a mixture of information and inspiration to attract potential applicants. Scot reads raw statistics pointing to our nation's educational crisis: "Fact: By the time they are nine, students in low-income areas are, on average, already three grade levels behind their peers in high-income areas in reading ability."

With a clear problem presented, Scot reminds his audience of Teach For America's mission. "You have gathered here tonight because of your interest in Teach For America. You have gathered because of your interest in building a movement among our nation's most promising future leaders."

Now on a roll, Scot poses a rhetorical question. "What will you get out of this? You will have the ability to make an immediate, direct, social impact after graduation. Not too many other employers can claim that. You will meet children who will learn something because you've taught them. Teach For America is not a commitment for one year, or two, but it is a lifelong commitment. You become part of a long-term network of individuals committed to the same cause. You will see your colleagues in jobs and positions where they can directly influence change. You will gain critical thinking skills. You will gain the ability to think on your feet, the ability to lead, and organizational skills."

"Now what are we looking for in candidates? Over time, Teach For America has found three skills that make a successful teacher. One, high achievement. We want to see that you have a sense of personal responsibility, that you have taken a leadership stance and that you have faced down challenges and sought out resources. Two, critical thinking. We need people who can stare at a problem and understand what levers to press to solve that problem. We want people who can overcome in spite of what are often very difficult circumstances. Three, constant learning. We want people who look to learn from resources outside of the traditional spheres."

Scot moves on through logistical information, explaining the lengthy application process and the two application deadlines in October and February. The barrage of questions starts. Someone asks if they need educational experience, or even experience working with children. Scot replies, "We seek applicants from all academic majors. No previous teaching experience is needed." "How competitive is Teach For America?" a nervous student asks. Scot waivers for a second, then replies, "I must be honest with you and tell you that Teach For America is highly competitive. But that's a good thing—we want to ensure our students get the most qualified, most committed teachers possible. Last year—2002—was unusual. Applications that year tripled from the previous year. We received 14,000 applications and filled 1,700 spots. That's an acceptance rate of about 13%. We think the huge rise in applications was influenced in some way by a weak economy and post–September 11th sentiments, after which many people returned to meaningful careers. The usual acceptance rate hovers around 25–28%."

Next comes the explanation of the assignment and placement. Upon interviewing, corps members rank twenty placements in three tiers: highly preferred, preferred, and not preferred. Ninety percent are placed in highly preferred sites, and 98% are placed in either preferred or highly preferred. "It's in Teach For America's interest to place you in a region where you want to be, where you will feel a tie to the community," Scot explains. Additionally, candidates rank their preference for teaching level, K–4, 5–8, or 9–12. "Here we ask for your flexibility and patience. So much of a placement boils down to district requirements. A district will look at your college transcript and have guidelines about who can teach in what position." Approximately 60% of corps members teach in elementary placements and 40% in secondary placements. Scot reiterates that districts hire corps members through alternate routes to teacher certification. Certification requirements depend on individual districts, though Teach For America has established partnerships with many states and schools of education, allowing corps members to take credentialing coursework or obtain a master's degree in education.

Scot discusses Teach For America's training, ongoing support, and financial information. "You will be sent to one of three summer institutes—in New York, Houston, or California. Your institute will be determined by where your teaching placement is. For four of those five weeks, you will be a summer school teacher. You will move kids from a failing level to a passing level. You are the teacher. Once you get to your site, we don't stop in terms of our influence. Teach For America continues to support you professionally through mentoring, learning teams, all-corps monthly meetings—just to name a few. We strive to place you in a school where there are already corps members in classrooms. You join a tight-knit group. It is a truly comprehensive experience." Last, Scot explains the financial ramifications of Teach For America. "We have tried to make this an experience that you cannot do based on financial reasons. Once you are in your school, you are paid in full by your school district, whether it be Oakland, New Orleans, or D.C. public schools. You are not working as a volunteer. In addition, we are a part of the Americorps Public Service program. You will earn over $9,000 in educational awards, which you may use retroactively for undergraduate loans, or to pay for credentialing programs or future graduate work. While you are in the classroom, you are eligible for loan forbearance on student loans. We provide need-based grants, to make this program possible for people who will accrue traveling and moving expenses."

Scot concludes with a last story, that of his fifth grader William, from whom Scot learned that "You have to be able to listen—listen to kids, principals, colleagues. You must take any advice you can get. Our kids deserve better. You, as a teacher, can always do better." On a final note, Scot delivers one last sales pitch. "Teach for two years. Join the force of leaders. Join the movement. Affect change." Scot thanks the audience for coming, and slowly people trickle out of the lecture hall and back into the rainy night.

Every year from September to February, information sessions like this take place on approximately three hundred college and university campuses nationwide. Undergraduates at top universities attend career fairs, where they stroll past booths offering high-paying corporate jobs, lucrative positions in the private sector. Yet these undergrads, in their newly pressed suits and clutching resumés, pause in front of the Teach For America booth, with its telltale red and blue banners and a mishmash of photographs, student work, and brochures which boast of corps members' accomplishments. There is almost certainly a line of people patiently waiting to speak with the Teach For America recruiter. They tell the recruiter things like, "I don't know much about you, but I had a friend who did Teach For America. She said it was the biggest challenge of her life," or "Do you hire engineering majors?"

These information sessions are hard sells; charismatic recruiters are given a detailed script to follow and are encouraged to share their own positive personal stories from Teach For America. There is much talk of the success of corps members and inspirational stories. There is little warning to interested applicants about exactly how demanding the two years are. There is little mention of the corps members who do not complete their commitments or leave the field of teaching after two years.

Teach For America has become a commonplace term among college campuses because of the organization's tremendous recruitment efforts, which focus on reaching the most talented and diverse seniors. Ten regional teams collaborate with the National Recruitment Team. Regional teams conduct campus visits to raise awareness and to build relationships with professors, deans, and students. Regional teams train and manage undergraduate and graduate campus recruiters, like Scot Fishman. The National Recruitment Team, based in Teach For

America's New York City office, is responsible for Internet marketing, marketing materials, and creating initiatives that target math, science, engineering applicants, as well as ensuring corps diversity. Many of Teach For America's best recruitment strategies come through word-of-mouth and alumni who return to their alma maters for recruitment efforts. Maureen Kay (1999, Washington, D.C.) joined recruitment efforts to "ensure that Teach For America attracts more minority applicants, as well as a better caliber of people."

Because of Teach For America's commitment to building a diverse organization, special attention is paid to recruiting candidates from various racial, ethnic, and socioeconomic backgrounds. Nationally at least 95% of the students that Teach For America reaches are African American and Latino. As such, Teach For America prioritizes the recruitment of people of color, with strong recruitment efforts at historically black colleges and universities and at all of *Hispanic Magazine*'s Top 25 Colleges for Hispanics. Teach For America advertises in media targeted at college students of color, and has built relationships with organizations that have a broad reach among students of color. To encourage people from all socioeconomic backgrounds, Teach For America offers financial aid programs, grants, and no-interest loans.

In spite of these efforts, some corps members question Teach For America's recruitment agenda. Serapha Reed (1995, New York) challenges Teach For America to rethink its pool of candidates:

> TFA must change its recruitment strategies if they want more corps members who are genuinely interested in creating an excellent education for all children and who teach for more than two years. By recruiting at elite (i.e. expensive) universities and favoring applicants who are planning to go on to law, government, or business programs, TFA makes their selection process seem more rigorous while, at the same time, attracting a group of applicants who are using TFA as a resumé builder and have no intention of working beyond their two year commitment in education. To think that one highly qualified corps member, with no experience in education, can create an excellent education for children in two years is

arrogant and self-righteous. There must be a focus on recruiting highly qualified corps members who come from families of low socioeconomic status and will likely stay in the field of education for longer than two years. All the sensitivity training in the world doesn't equal real life experiences with the physical, psychological, and emotional effects of poverty. In the literature of TFA, the organization writes about being a diverse corps and wanting to be even more diverse. Yet, with all the statistics kept on demographics, none are kept on the economic status of the families that corps members come from and it is never addressed as a concern. It is not enough to recruit people of color, if the majority come from suburban, middle-high income families and go to the most elite schools. Obviously, TFA should continue to recruit people of color as race is still often an indicator of class in the United States. At the same time, TFA should target highly qualified candidates of lower socioeconomic backgrounds and of all ethnicities who have first hand experience that is pertinent to the experiences of their future students. However, because of TFA's recruitment strategies, the corps is largely made up of European Americans, who seemingly come from well-to-do families and have had many educational opportunities. The result is patronizing and ineffective: pity for the students they teach and self-conceit for having "survived" in some of this country's poorest school systems.

Teach For America is often regarded as an elitist organization. As the Recruitment Director of the Midwestern region from 2000–2002, Nakia Whitney (1996, New Jersey) worked to dispel this misconception:

In my experience spreading the word of Teach For America on college and university campuses, it was perceived as elitist. The organization is looking to recruit the cream of the crop, the movers and shakers of campuses. I got the sense that people of color didn't always feel like they would fit the TFA definition of mover and shaker. This prevented people of color from applying. If you look at the numbers of people of color who fit that mold, it's much smaller than their white counterparts. Also many people of color questioned the true motives behind this organization that puts highly educated, young white people into poor black and Latino communities for a short period of time. It made me realize how difficult it is to recruit people of color, why many people of color don't apply, and why even fewer matriculate.

To demonstrate its commitment to diversity, Teach For America points to its self-compiled statistics. In the 2002 corps, 38% identify themselves as people of color. This number exceeds the 22% of college grads who are people of color and the national teacher pool of approximately 12% people of color. Thirteen percent of the 2002 corps identify themselves as African Americans, well above the national average of 8.7 percent African-American college graduates. However, the elitist image may be self-perpetuated. In a 2003 press release, Teach For America boasted of the high credentials and selective backgrounds of its applicants, "The organization drew more than seven percent of the University of Chicago class of 2003 and six percent of seniors from Northwestern University and Georgetown University."

Building on the recruitment effort, the admissions team has the enormous responsibility of selecting the corps. The admission process begins with an extensive written application, including letters of recommendation, letters of intent, and reflective essays. The most promising candidates, approximately 70%–80% of all applicants, are invited for a day-long interview. The interview includes a sample teaching lesson, a group interview, and a personal interview. All applicants are interviewed with the same pool of questions and evaluated on one comprehensive rubric, to view the applicant through many lenses. The majority of people who apply are rejected, with an overall acceptance rate of approximately 20%.

The results are a diverse corps with notable academic credentials and high accolades. Take, for instance, the 2002 corps. The 1,731 members of the 2002 corps came from 395 universities, over 600 cities, and all 50 states and the District of Columbia. (Because of Teach For America's affiliation with Americorps, corps members must be citizens, nationals, or lawful permanent United States residents.) In the 2002 corps, the average GPA was 3.5 and the average SAT self-reported score was 1310. Eighty-nine percent of corps members reported to have held leadership roles in their undergraduate universities.

It is nearly impossible to point to one universal explanation for why so many people, from such varied backgrounds, come to Teach For America. Many corps members see their joining as accidental or solely by chance—stumbling upon Teach For America or seeing flyers posted around campus. Many realize that their post-college plans are uncertain, like Dennis Guikema (1994, Bay Area), who saw graduation as "a juncture in my life where I was looking out over a cliff, over the edge, and I didn't see where it would go." Others use Teach For America as a way to navigate through confusing certification requirements and lengthy credential programs. Many responses touch on Teach For America's public service roots, the desire to bring about change, and the opportunity to join a nationwide movement.

social justice

Though Teach For America corps members are not volunteers, there is a strong link to public service efforts in the minds of corps members. The altruistic corps member sees Teach For America as a means to bring about social justice. Take, for instance, Caitlin Wittig (1997, Rio Grande Valley), who viewed Teach For America as "a political way to be proactive about social justice." Mark McClinchie (1996, Houston) abandoned his original post-grad plans to enter the military to join Teach For America, "I joined to pursue social justice opportunities rather than contribute to social injustice." In fact, many corps members reported that their backgrounds in community service led them to see Teach For America as a natural progression.

Heidi Austin (2002, North Carolina) came to Teach For America because of her interest in working with a service-oriented organization.

> Throughout high school and college, all I wanted to do was join the Peace Corps. In the fall of 2001, I began my work with the Peace Corps in

Turkmenistan. Two days after arriving, September 11th happened and the Peace Corps evacuated all its volunteers from Central Asia. I found out about Teach For America through the Peace Corps, and it seemed to fit into my ideals of spending time with a service-oriented project.

Murray Carlisle (1997, Mississippi Delta) came from a similar community-service background. As an Americorps member, Murray worked from 1996 to 1997 as a teaching assistant in an English as a Second Language (ESL) classroom. Similarly, Teach For America appealed to Danielle DeLancey's (2002, North Carolina) dual interest in community service and urban schools. "As an undergrad, I was introduced to urban poverty by tutoring at an inner-city school in Nashville. Mostly I joined TFA because I agree 100% with its mission."

Not only did Teach For America's social service realm appeal to Stephanie Crement (1999, East Palo Alto), but equally enticing was the opportunity to work proactively: "Upon graduating, I was exploring several service-oriented programs. A lot of them felt reactive, like they were fixing problems that were already created. Teaching felt proactive." Chris Barbic (1992, Houston) voiced a similar sentiment, "There is problem identification and there's problem solution. Too often all we have is problem identification, pointing out what's not working. I joined TFA because of its problem solution capacity." Meghan Corman (2002, Los Angeles) grew up in a family where social service was an embedded value. "My mother always told me to take what you're good at and use it for the people who need it most." Teach For America was the ideal combination of her interests in social change and literacy development. "I joined Teach For America kind of hoping to find out that I'd teach as a career."

Before teaching, Matthew Schmitt (1999, New Orleans) had worked with adolescent boys serving time in juvenile detention. There he witnessed the feelings of hopelessness that children, already at the age of fourteen, felt about their dim futures. Being privy to this end of the spectrum led Matthew to teaching:

I had been drawn to teaching because of a natural progression. Having worked at the Boysville Juvenile Correctional Facility in Clinton Township, Michigan, I felt like I had to teach. The guys would ask me why school had never come alive for them, why every teacher had told them they were failures. I joined Teach For America to try to figure that out. I went into teaching to try to find the poetry in children before it was stomped out of them. I went to teach so that I could learn how any child could end up in a detention center, and to do my part to prevent it.

providing educational opportunity

Other corps members link their decision to join Teach For America to the negative or positive education they received in their upbringing. Mike Garcia (2002, Baltimore) had a unique experience. Growing up in the Rio Grande Valley of South Texas, Mike fondly remembered the young, energetic teachers he had in high school.

> They were fresh out of college. They were excited and arrived with great ideas. They understood us as students. We felt comfortable with them. They wanted me to become a critical thinker and to work towards my future. They made me see that I had options outside of the poverty of South Texas. They constantly pushed and encouraged me, sending messages of "You can do it. You will do it. Let no one stop you." It was extraordinary to have a teacher who cared and who had such a huge impact on my life.

Mike was the first member of his immediate and extended family to attend college.

> At first my family was reluctant. They didn't want me to go far away, and it was so expensive. Those teachers told me otherwise. They told me to do what I felt in my heart. They told me that I could do as much with my life as I wanted to do.

As an undergrad at the University of Michigan, Mike stumbled across a flyer for Teach For America and went online to research the program. "It sounded so familiar. I thought I had heard of it." Through investigating Teach For America's long history of placement in South Texas and consulting with his parents still in South Texas, Mike began to wonder whether his favorite high school teachers were Teach For America corps members themselves. Mike has not yet been able to determine whether his teachers were in fact part of Teach For America. The subject was addressed in a CNN documentary aired in December 2002, in which camera crews followed Mike through the first months of his Teach For America commitment.

Mike saw his teachers as his reason for making the commitment. "The more I thought about the impact my teachers had on me, the more I identified the impact I wanted to have on my students." Mike applied his unique perspective directly to his first grade students. "I came into teaching knowing firsthand what students from poor communities are going through." Just as his teachers made him excited for school, Mike tried to do the same for his students.

> These kids look up to us as teachers. Every time I tell a student "Good job" or "Keep it up," they get the message that they are smart, that they can succeed. Too often encouraging words, constant praise and rewards are taken for granted.

In his first year of teaching, Mike set the goal of having all of his first grade students complete the year at a second grade reading level. He relied on song and dance as a meaningful way to instruct students on phonemic awareness, numbers, colors, shapes, and counting. His ultimate goal was for his students to leave his classroom two grade levels above where they should be.

Allison Serafin (2000, Houston) joined Teach For America in hopes of being the teacher she never had. "Growing up in Houston, I dropped out of high school and earned my GED. I became very familiar with what it is like to be considered at risk." She believed that this awareness of public education from her own background lead her to Teach For America. Then there is Amy Jennings (1997, Southern Louisiana), the daughter of two immigrant parents who very much valued public education as the cornerstone of democracy. "My father was in the Air Force and I, as a result, was a student in twenty-three different schools. I saw so much educational inequity as I was growing up that already I had this sense of the education I received being subpar." At the age of twelve, Amy began to ask questions like "How come education systems can be so bad under our nation's democracy?" and "How can I contribute to improving our democracy through education?" Coincidentally, at the time when Amy was grappling with these issues, her family moved out of a house into which six Los Angeles Teach For America members were moving in. In the transition of moving, Amy remembers spending time with them, seeing their efforts for educational reform, and setting her sights on joining Teach For America herself.

Compare these accounts to Payton Carter (1999, Bay Area), who attended a diverse public high school in Seattle that was considered to be "the shining star of what public education could be." Payton's desire to teach stemmed from his gratitude for his own good fortune. Brent Maddin (1999, Southern Louisiana) opted for a rural placement because of his own rural education: "One of the factors that shaped me was my own rural education. I joined Teach For America because I felt I could be a teacher to shape my students." Paul Holloman (1998, North Carolina) returned to his home state of North Carolina to strengthen the community that had educated him. He described his own high school experience as "bipolar," switching from the educational extremes of a particularly troubled high school to graduating from arguably one of the nation's best science and math magnet high schools. This experience raised his awareness of educational inequity, but his real motivation for joining Teach For America was the chance to be surrounded by motivated students and inspiring teachers:

> I joined Teach For America because I felt like I wanted to give back to
> the state of North Carolina for what money the taxpayers had invested

in my education. I had seen schools on both extremes and I knew in North Carolina there were schools that needed teachers committed to making a difference in the lives of kids. I felt Teach For America could really put me in a position to have that impact.

Carissa Nauman (2000, North Carolina) always wanted to teach and discovered Teach For America through an Internet search. She turned for advice to her favorite high school teacher. "My teacher told me to go for it—this was the way I should go. I was passionate about education because of this one special teacher. I wanted to try to pay back this teacher by being that person for one of my future students."

> *Children in low-income areas needed me. Corporate America didn't need me.*
>
> —Lisa Leadbitter (1997, Houston)

a pathway into teaching

In a day and age where teaching requires jumping over obstacles of confusing credentialing programs and expensive coursework, Teach For America smoothes the pathway into the classroom. Sarah Fang (1996, Phoenix) wanted to try teaching, but wasn't interested in investing the time and money into a credential without having some classroom exposure, "TFA was a non-committal way into the profession. It gave me the chance to try teaching and to decide where to go from there." Eight years later, Sarah is still teaching.

Alan Giuliani came to Teach For America at the age of twenty, upon graduating from New Mexico State University. Immediately Alan believed himself to be like many other corps members in that he sort of "stumbled into TFA." He pointed to his lifelong love of school and academics as the key reason for his commitment. "I had always loved school and learning and everything associated with school. Not only did I have no other burning desires professionally, but I didn't really know of any other careers that would suit me." However, rather than pursuing teaching through a traditional route, Alan saw Teach For America as the most efficient way into the classroom. "My dad told me not to waste my time in education school, that there were ways to go into teaching without all that coursework, all those requirements."

the mission

Teach For America's mission entices the idealistic college graduate, like Nancy Taylor (1999, Rio Grande Valley), who felt Teach For America epitomized all her beliefs. Christina Kelley (1994, North Carolina) recognized her own youthful energy: "I grew up wanting to save the world. TFA tapped into my idealism." Amy Christie (2001, New York) came to Teach For America with the ambition of making a difference:

> In college, I took a few undergraduate education classes, and was totally drawn to one class, "Growing Up American," which looked at issues in urban education. I found out about TFA through the professor of that class, and right away I bought into its idealism. I liked the idea that if you are passionate enough about something, you can make a difference.

Much of Teach For America's appeal comes in its being a widespread movement, effecting change in classrooms nationwide, as revealed by Wendy Eberhart (2000, North Carolina): "Coming out of Brown University, I knew I wanted to teach. I was drawn to Teach For America because I liked the idea of being a part of this broader movement that went beyond the walls of my individual classroom."

> *I was disturbed and concerned about the quality of education. It was a chance to pursue a passion I had in teaching as well as working closely with the educational process in schools.*
>
> —**Ray Owens (1990, Los Angeles)**

Laura Perkins (1999, Bay Area) came to Teach For America with her undergraduate degree in public policy from Duke University. She realized that although policy would allow her to effect change at the higher level, that level was too removed from change at the grassroots level. Additionally, she saw the growing chasm between those who make policy and those who live on a day-to-day basis with those policies.

> I quickly realized that educational policy decisions were crafted by people who didn't understand how the system worked, at the school level. Their ideas weren't feasible. If I wanted to work on educational policy, I needed to be in the schools that needed help.

Xanthe Jory (1996, New York) thought that a career in education would provide the best opportunity to make an impact on a community in which she was invested. She joined Teach For America after working for a South Bronx organization that focused on community development. "It wasn't a nice place to work. I wasn't able to make an impact, either as an individual or through the organization. But it caused me to think about the problems I saw in that inner-city community and I realized that education seemed to be the root of many of them."

These Teach For America corps members come into schools believing that with their college degrees and their good intentions, they have the ability to make a difference. Teach For America has sold them on brochure platitudes, offering them the chance to address social injustice and to change the life prospects of at-risk students. But with those altruistic motivations comes an idealistic naivety that is immediately put to the test on the first day of class. In making the commitment to Teach For America, corps members may be quick to dismiss the realizations of Hillary Roselund (1999, Washington, D.C.), "I was blown away by how hard teaching was."

chapter three

the summer institute

The purpose of the institute is to prepare you to lead your students to achieve significant academic gains. You will teach summer school students in Houston or New York and will attend professional development workshops in the evenings. While no pre-service training program of any length can provide you with all that you need to know to excel as a teacher, the institute aims to provide you with a solid foundation of the skills and knowledge you will need to effect dramatic academic gains in your classroom. At the same time, the institute—and Teach For America's entire Training & Support program—is designed to supplement your own initiative to advance your professional development over time.

—Foreword to the 2002 Teach For America summer institute packet, sent to all incoming corps members

At 6:30 on a July morning in Houston, Texas, the thermometer climbs above ninety degrees. Moody Towers, twin high-rise dormitories in the central campus of the University of Houston, are a flurry of activity. Hundreds of twenty-something-year-olds wake up, stumble to the bathrooms, dress in business attire, wait for elevators to take them downstairs to the cafeteria, where they grab bagged lunches. They filter out to the early morning heat and board a brigade of school buses.

The buses chug their ways to elementary, middle, and high schools in Houston's low-income neighborhoods, where the same twenty-something-year-olds disembark to begin another day of work at Teach For America's summer institute.

Four hours later, the hallways of Houston schools are filled with students and their young teachers. The students have come because they failed end-of-year standardized tests or to make up credits to be promoted to the next grade. The teachers have come to gain practical, hands-on classroom experience while applying theoretical and pedagogical approaches. For the teachers, the school day is non-stop action—a juggling act of teaching, meeting with faculty advisors, and observing their fellow teachers in action; attending training sessions addressing literacy instruction, students with special needs, and diversity and cultural awareness.

At eleven at night, the day is far from over for Teach For America corps members. T-shirts and shorts replace neckties and skirts, but these young teachers don't expect to return to their dorm rooms for a few more hours. They attend seminars on how to address different learning modalities or how to integrate music into the elementary school classroom. At the computer lab, corps members type up revised lesson plans. The dormitory lounges are crammed with corps members discussing tomorrow's lesson plans. They rest in cushy chairs while reading articles about multicultural approaches to teaching or about child development. They meet with mentor teachers to reflect on another day of teaching, how their lesson on Cesar Chavez flopped, or what to do when José won't stop talking during silent reading. Shuttle buses pick up and drop off corps members at Kinko's, where the line to copy geography worksheets and math quizzes goes out the door. Late into the night or in the early hours of the morning, corps members quietly find a stopping point for their work and, out of sheer exhaustion, call it a day. They disappear into dorm rooms for a few hours of sleep before beginning again the next day.

This is the frenzy of Teach For America's summer institute, the critical five-week pre-service program to prepare corps members for their placements. To an outsider, this gathering may appear to be a continuation of college or some twisted version of summer camp—with hundreds of recent grads housed in dormitories and the average age hovering around twenty-three. However, this is a far cry from college life. These college graduates are to be transformed into teachers, ready to take on some of the nation's most challenging classroom placements. The summer institute is notoriously difficult, with busy schedules of training and preparation. Amid complaints about the endless work, corps members often regard institute as "teaching boot camp." The days are long and the work is never-ending, for there is much to be done. Here recent grads take on an enormous responsibility: becoming a Teach For America corps member in the struggle for educational equity.

The summer institute's importance cannot be stressed enough; since it is one of the most visible components of the organization, critics often point to its brevity as one of Teach For America's most prevalent flaws. In a 1992 *Educational Horizons* article, author Gary Clabaugh stated:

> Discarding the thoughtful, thorough and progressive preparation characteristics of all expert professions, Teach For America coaxes half-committed aspirants through just five weeks of summer crash work in pedagogy. . . . From ignorance to competence in just thirty days of preparation!

Criticism also comes from within the corps itself, for example, Jay Hartling (2002, Baltimore), who called the institute "extremely disorganized" and saw material as "not relevant to the classroom." Serapha Reed (1995, New York) explained ineffective usage of time, a hazy summer school curriculum, and a withholding of teaching materials forces corps members to "reinvent the wheel":

> Currently corps members are told to come up with lesson plans on their own and are given teacher guides and teacher's editions only as a reference. Therefore, they spend a lot of time trying to come up with lesson

plans that dazzle from scratch. Many find this task very challenging. If corps members were given a curriculum, they could focus on how to deliver it effectively and, at the same time, manage the classroom. Several days of summer school learning are wasted because corps members, with no prior educational background, don't know the developmental or educational needs of the children they are teaching. By the time corps members figure out what their students need to know, summer school is almost over. It is unnecessary and arrogant of TFA to assume that new corps member, with no educational background, can develop better lesson plans than the educators who write teacher guides.

In June 1990, Teach For America opened the doors to its first-ever summer institute, with 504 corps members training for eight weeks at University of Southern California. As David Wakelyn (1990, Los Angeles) explained, "It was a chaotic time. We were building an airplane while we were trying to fly it." Charter corps member James Sparkman (1990, New York) reflected on the palpable energy of the first-ever corps:

> When we arrived at the University of Southern California in the summer of 1990, it was the very first meeting of Teach For America. Five hundred of us piled into the auditorium. We didn't know each other. We didn't know who this Wendy Kopp person was. All of a sudden, Wendy got on stage and a chant broke out. The entire auditorium was chanting "*TFA. TFA.*" Nobody scripted it. It just broke out. It was a phenomenal, phenomenal thing. We all believed in this thing that joined us all together. It was the most amazing thing in the world. I'll never forget it.

At the time, the institute gave an abbreviated sense of education school programs, with the classic student-teaching experience in Los Angeles' year-round schools, under the watchful leadership of a master teacher. When not in class, corps members attended workshops and received feedback from educational experts, who averaged twenty years of classroom experience.

Teach For America closed the first summer institute with the parting words of Ray Owens (1990, Los Angeles):

It is with a good deal of reservation and humility that I stand before you, my colleagues, TFA staff, faculty, family, and friends . . .

Far too many of the children we will encounter have decided that the American dream is an eternal nightmare. The monsters of educational failure have locked them into the dismal dens of ignorance and despair. They have internalized the low level of expectation and inferiority that many of this nation's school systems have designed and perpetuated for them. America has said to these children that their dreams must be deferred. . . . The nation that promises "liberty and justice for all" has failed these children by sending them to schools that don't offer courses in calculus and literary analysis, courses that they will need in order to prepare for the demanding coursework of our institutions of higher learning. The country where "all men [and women] are created equal" has said to these children that they are an exception to this rule by consistently allowing unequal educational opportunities to exist between the haves and the have-nots . . .

In these classrooms it will not matter that you are a Phi Beta Kappa. The children in Compton or rural Georgia may not be impressed that you attended a prestigious university. What will matter will be your ability to earn the respect and admiration of your students. These children need our genuine compassion and respect. That means that we will have to show them that we care and that we believe in them. . . . Saying it will just not be enough. We must show it in the way we look at them. . . . We must show it in the way that we encourage them . . . And we must show it in the way that we work relentlessly on their behalf. . . .

We should believe that we have as much to learn from our students as they have to learn from us. Each one of them has an experience. . . . Each one of them has a story. We must learn that experience and listen to that story. For, embodied in these stories—embedded in these experiences—is the history of our nation and our world. Sometimes it will tell an unpleasant story. But it is one that we must contend with. Sometimes it will tell the story of the brutal boot of oppression that has trampled the culture and spirit of many marginalized groups in our country. Yet, until we have these truths, until we face these children, we can never begin to eradicate the wrongs that still exist . . .

I leave this institute with fresh hope . . . a hope that is rooted in a belief that when people care enough and believe enough that they really can make a difference. I challenge you to care . . . I challenge you to believe today. There is a little girl in Baton Rouge who needs to know that you care. There is a little boy in Compton who needs to know that you believe in him. We must all realize our vested interest in this project. Whatever our differences may be, now we must come together on the issue of providing the best possible education to the young people of this nation.

When the school bell rings on day one and all our students are in their seats, we will hold the future of this nation and this world in our hands. Whatever we do will have lasting implications, not only on the lives of those students, but also on the lives of all those who they come in contact with. So then, the question that we should ask ourselves should not be, "How can I make this work?" The question must be, "How can I afford not to make this work?"

The Teach For America charter corps headed to classrooms in Los Angeles, New York City, New Orleans, Baton Rouge, Eastern North Carolina, and rural Georgia. However, corps members were not shy in voicing their complaints. David Wakelyn (1990, Los Angeles) felt that his training focused too much on pedagogy while it glossed over hands-on practical information.

The training seemed to be grounded in this assumption that if we were all multicultural in our approaches, that that would take care of things. Kids need to see themselves in the curriculum, but first, they need someone who can show them how to master fractions and complex problem solving.

Scott Joftus (1990, New York) recalled the following:

> There was so much excitement at the 1990 institute. We had the men-
> tality of being pioneers. We were comparing ourselves to the birth of
> the Peace Corps. But at the end of it, we felt like we were unleashed to
> teach with so little tangible information about classroom management
> and effective approaches to content.

Corps members simply did not feel ready to take on their own classrooms.

As corps members complained, criticism flooded in from outside of
the corps. The central debate pertained to whether Teach For America
was contributing to the demoralization of the teaching profession.
Critics pointed out that by creating backdoors into the classroom, Teach
For America fed into the misconception that bright people, with little
more than a college degree, were qualified to become effective teachers—
a theory with the nickname "Just let 'em teach." University of Illinois at
Urbana-Champaign professor Cameron McCarthy was one of the first
researchers to look critically at Teach For America. Affiliated with the
Wisconsin Center for Educational Research, McCarthy examined Teach
For America's first-ever summer institute. He was struck by what he
viewed as "an arrogant approach to the status quo in teacher education,
TFA's insufficient training, and its impending disillusionment."

> Right away, I gained a sense that this was a deeply ideological program
> invested in making an effective commitment to social change. It struck
> me as being such a voluntary, altruistic commitment, similar to the
> Peace Corps, almost like the Green Berets, committed to saving the
> country from within. However, as I spent time looking at the training
> of corps members, I believed this to be a program that was vastly inade-
> quate to meet the needs of educating our nation's youth. Teach For
> America seemed to rise out of this demonstration against the establish-
> ment, against the bureaucratic codes of traditional teacher training. In
> this idealistic arrogance, Teach For America seemed to want to hack the

teacher training process down to the bare essentials, to show the fluff in traditional credential programs. At its inception, Teach For America presented itself to practitioners as arrogant.

Professor McCarthy's critique came at an organizational level, and was not directed at the motives of individual corps members:

> Teach For America corps members had a strong desire to do something. They entered the profession certainly with a degree of idealism, but also with this confidence that because of their high GPAs from reputable universities they would innately be able to deliver within the classroom. In many cases, the corps members found the going to be very difficult, and they dropped out. Our research pointed out considerable and rapid disillusionment. This was a group of well-intentioned, very bright, very young people committed to a cause, and they met various levels of frustration.

Dissension also came from within the Teach For America staff. In 1990, Jim Lerman joined the Teach For America team as the Director of Professional Development. He worked to set up the institute and to train its faculty. His position lasted only six months; he believes he was asked to leave because "his views about corps member training conflicted with those of the larger organization."

> I believed, and I still believe, that there is a body of knowledge that corps members needed to know about teaching. Teach For America needed to say with some degree of assurance that they were producing a corps of people who had knowledge and confidence about teaching and about learning. Teach For America has a responsibility to build into corps members as much professional knowledge as possible, and that simply can't be done in a five-week stint.

Corps member David Wakelyn (1990, Los Angeles) agreed about the ill effects of Teach For America on the professionalization of teaching:

Teach For America's main flaw is that it does nothing, absolutely nothing to change the fact that teaching remains a semi-profession. The TFA leadership doesn't believe that there's an expert body of knowledge that takes time to develop, thereby upholding the notion that great teachers are born, not made. Rather than being an ally with the forces who seek to improve teaching as a profession, it has been an antagonist. That's a shame. A real moment—to take a stab at improving the conditions of teaching—has been lost here.

Since that first summer, Teach For America continues to seek the most effective, if short-term, training. An enormous change came in 1994, when Teach For America adopted a new format for the summer institute, due to both budgetary restraints and efforts to improve training. Teach For America teamed up with the Houston Independent School District to teach summer school students in ten of Houston's elementary, middle, and high schools. To prepare corps members, Teach For America adopted a collaborative model, which is still used today. Corps members in groups of four are responsible for teaching a summer-school classroom. "We wanted corps members to find systems and instructional programs themselves, but at the same time be instructed in what we thought was the best way," explained former Institute Director Karolyn Belcher (1990, New Orleans). TFA realized that the best possible mentors came from within the corps, rather than the external educational experts and teacher trainers. Teach For America created the position of a Corps Member Advisor (CMA), a second-year corps member or alumni to train of a group of twelve new corps members. The 1994 model of the institute has undergone many revisions and improvements, but is the general model still in use today.

To fully prepare for the institute, Teach For America starts the planning well before the summer. In working as the Director for Institute Operation from 1996 to 1999, Donald Kamentz collaborated with the Houston Independent School District to cultivate school relationships and prove Teach For America's commitment to the district. School Directors are hired in the early winter and regularly meet and conference about basic curriculum, organizational expectations, and goals for corps members. The remainder of the institute staff—Corps Member Advisors, Literacy Consultants, and Curriculum Specialists— is hired in the early spring and meets school directors during a weekend conference. School teams plan additional conference phone calls to prepare for the summer. Staff arrives up to a week before corps members descend on the institute.

Teacher training involves much more than simply reading instruction and classroom management. Teach For America must create a sensitive corps who understand how issues of race, ethnicity, and socioeconomics impact students' learning styles and environments. Corps members discuss how poverty may be an obstacle to student achievement. In breakout sessions and affinity groups, Teach For America encourages open dialogues about diversity issues. As cultural sensitivity is woven into every aspect of the curriculum, Teach For America sends the message that corps members must consider race, ethnicity, and socioeconomics in instructional planning, establishing classroom management, curriculum delivery, and working within communities and schools. This pressing area continues to be where Teach For America spends much of its time readdressing and revamping curriculum.

In the drive for accountability in the mid-1990s, Teach For America pushed corps members to focus on promoting significant academic gains for their students. Just as school districts relied on standardized test scores to assess student achievement, Teach For America relied on empirical data to measure the progress corps members and their students made in the classroom. Karolyn Belcher (1990, New Orleans) explained the rationale for accountability:

> We found that our most successful corps members were able to articulate their goals regarding at what level their students came in and where they wanted to go. At that point we realized that measurable student achievement needed to be the clarity of our focus and an integral part of our vocabulary.

When referring to student achievement, Teach For America mostly looks at results from standardized test scores. Steven Farr, the Vice President of Program and Design (1993, Rio Grande Valley), stated the following:

> Significant academic gains became a sort of rally point for our staff and corps members. We began to think critically in our own implementation of this principle. We tried to answer the question of what went into the success of our corps members who were really increasing student achievement reflected by standardized test scores.

In 1999, Abigail Smith (1992, North Carolina) took over as Institute Director. Her immediate challenge was to maximize the five-week period without an overly stressful or chaotic environment. In 2000, Abigail and the Teach For America team advocated a significant staffing change, the addition of Curriculum Specialists. The positions emerged to relieve the demand on CMAs. Curriculum Specialists present the core curriculum to corps members in every school, boost staff morale, and increase the quality of curriculum delivery. In an intense but manageable institute, corps members are asked to rate the institute's pace on a scale from overwhelming to manageable. Teach For America encourages corps members to set their own limits to maintain healthy lifestyles.

Last, Teach For America realizes the shortcomings of a five-week training program and conveys the departing message that corps members need to actively seek out resources and professional development programs. Abigail Smith explained, "The institute gives corps members the fundamental skills and information they need. We leave them with the ethic that no one can learn it all in five weeks. It is then their responsibility to continue their teaching as a reflective practice."

In 2001, with a growing number of corps members, Teach For America created a second summer institute in New York. The decision came from an organizational feeling that the quality of instruction would decline as numbers rose. In summer 2003, Teach For America expanded to three institutes in Houston, New York, and Los Angeles.

Voices from within the corps differ with regard to the effectiveness of the summer institute. Almost unanimously corps members agree on the nature of the dilemma: How—in five short weeks—can corps members be effectively trained to take on such challenging positions? Wendy Eberhart (2000, North Carolina) wondered, "How in the world can you do it all in five weeks?" Disagreement arises, however, when corps members are asked to reflect about how well prepared they were for their classrooms.

First, many corps members are satisfied that the institute was an adequate preparation for the field of teaching. Allison Serafin (2001, Houston) commented, "The institute prepared us as best as it could. It was a trial by fire. That's sort of the nature of teaching." For the bulk of corps members, the institute is their first avenue into the classroom and the first chance to stand in front of students and execute lesson plans. Part of its value lies in its sheer exposure to teaching and a forum to test out new teaching personas. Though she had previous coursework in education, Kate Driscoll (1998, Washington, D.C.) appreciated the practicality of the institute: "I left Houston knowing what I needed to do. I got answers to questions I had. I got a sense of what I was getting into." The institute gave Danielle DeLancey (2002, North Carolina) a sense of her own mistakes and what practices to avoid in her later placement, "I felt like I was being thrown to the wolves. Yet it was such a steep learning curve and that's what prepared me. Mostly I had a model of what I didn't want my class to be, so I worked off of that."

> *The institute comes as a shocking experience. Life is no longer about you; it's about your students.*
>
> —Mike Fisher (1999, Rio Grande Valley)

The institute often overwhelms in the sheer volume of resources and opportunities it presents, including workshops, seminars, mentoring, and support groups. Corps members who are satisfied with their institute experience often arrive ready to take advantage of the endless possibilities. Amy Christie (2001, New York) descended upon the first-ever New York institute "like a sponge, ready to absorb everything I could learn, ready to be proactive." Moreover corps members, like Heidi Austin (2002, North Carolina), come to appreciate the work ethic that is a fabric of the institute. "The institute overstresses you. You work long hours, but it makes you ready for your placement, in that when you get to your site and really start working hard, you're not so shocked." Maureen Kay's (1999, Washington, D.C.) appreciation for the institute came on a personal level, as well as professional:

> The institute was hectic and stressful but at the same time, I was learning so much, using an entirely new vocabulary and new tools. The institute prepared me emotionally for what I'd be in for. I was really prepared for the feelings of stress, the feeling of being overwhelmed, the need to constantly think about the next thing.

The institute is also the first time in the Teach For America journey that corps members face disillusionment. Amy Way (1998, Washington, D.C.) finished her work at the institute "frustrated and a bit fearful that I wouldn't make an impact through Teach For America. I was ready to not do it. Ultimately, I didn't quit because of the idea of commitment. But I felt that at the institute, I was pushed so hard that I thought I wouldn't be able to make an impact. It was discouraging, to realize how much there was to do and how much I'd be taking on."

Another enormous benefit is the social and emotional support network that not only carries corps members through five weeks in the summer, but is applied in regions nationwide. The institute links the diverse, intelligent, and passionate individuals who make up the national corps. Rob Reich (1992, Houston) explained, "You meet people who are in the same boat as you. They become your social and emotional support. Those relationships help you get through your first year."

Payton Carter (1999, Bay Area) gave a comprehensive overview of the institute:

It was a ridiculous experience. With teaching full time and reading and discussing education theory, I slept on average four hours a night. On top of that, there were one thousand of us in one giant dormitory, so we spent an inordinate amount of time socializing and networking.

Though I got a lot out of it, there is a limit to the amount that you can learn in such a crazy environment. Halfway through, I think my brain got overloaded, and I stopped picking up new things.

But by the institute being so rigorous, two things happen. First, you set extremely high expectations for yourself as a teacher. Second, it makes you become diligent in time management. It was such a challenge and an accomplishment to finish the institute, that when I started my teaching assignment, I was surprised by how much free time I had.

Corps members who staunchly believe that Teach for American failed to adequately train them voice complaints about the practicality of the institute and how unrealistic teaching scenarios are. During the summer, corps members teach an average of one hour a day to a small group of students, which is very different than the realities of teaching large classes for eight straight hours. Another concern pertains to actual teaching placements, which may not mirror what corps members will teach in the fall. Though Teach For America does its best to make teaching assignments mirror permanent placements, this isn't always feasible. For example, Susannah Nichols (2002, Detroit) taught a kindergarten classroom at the institute, and was placed in a fourth grade classroom when she arrived at her region. The practical teaching strategies that she acquired over the summer were "useless" when it came time to apply them to her upper elementary placement. Melissa Dyckes Storm (1994, Southern Louisiana) stated, "My institute, in 1994, was not effective at all. I taught a group of self-motivated students, who had chosen to come to summer school. We spent the summer reading plays and writing poetry. It was a totally unrealistic experience and did nothing to prepare me for my placement."

I got more of a badge of courage out of the institute than actual strate-
gies to take to my classroom.

—Justin Arnold (2001, Los Angeles)

Much of the criticism from within the corps pertains to the culture which the institute breeds. Disenchantment often strikes in the third week, when corps members come to resent the high stress and long hours. Susannah Nichols (2002, Detroit) pointed out "the pressurized environment in which people get disillusioned with the process." Arlen Carey (1999, Southern Louisiana) took issue with the treatment of corps members:

> The 1999 Institute felt like a fraternity initiation for me. There seemed to be these messages coming from above of, "Let's see how bad we can make it for you. If you quit, you're a wimp. You need to tough it out." It became an endurance test and seemed totally unnecessary to me. I felt like their training went against my personal orientation of mutual respect and the way people should be treated.

Arlen believed that because of the long hours of the institute, he arrived at his placement tired and already burned out.

Yet additional criticism from corps members pertains to the misdi-rected agenda of the summer institute. Corps members state that diversity issues too often take the place of the need for more practical information, like math instruction. William Jacobs (2001, New Mexico) stated "the institute has to address how to raise student achievement every day all day. Teach For America needs to provide a more practical approach so that corps members are ready to teach math as well as ready to address African-American learning modalities." Jay Hartling's (2002, Baltimore) grievances focus on the program's misconstrued priorities:

> I felt like the priority was moving this political agenda of Teach For America's sensitivity to political and cultural diversity. Not enough pri-ority was put on instructing the students of New York and not making

corps members ready to take up their placements. In terms of the material presented, I couldn't digest it all. There was simply no time to read it and it wasn't relevant to the classroom. We didn't discuss enough, if any, teaching techniques; instead the majority of discussions dealt with cultural sensitivity and how we felt about diversity—race, sexual orientation, gender.

Criticism from Gary Rubinstein (1991, Houston) pertains to the evolution of the institute. He is a product of the first model of the institute, in which a wide range of educational specialists—master teachers, principals, veteran teachers in the classroom for twenty years—served on staff. Gary regards the 1991 institute as "better than the ones that happen nowadays. We were trained by the best of the best. The expertise was astonishing. They had so much experience." In its present form, Gary finds that TFA alumni, now in leadership positions, paint too rosy a picture of what corps members are about to face. Gary urges Teach For America to rely on the institute leadership from a combination of different types of alumni—"the first-year dynamo, and the people who struggle because they are not dynamos but who manage to do a good job anyway, and also a lot of non-TFA veterans." He explained:

> When Teach For America shifted away from training by educational experts and hiring alumni to train the incoming corps, they lost their diversity. Too often Teach For America thinks of diversity in terms of race and ethnicity. But diversity is people with different opinions. With alums staffing the institute, diversity was gone and the institute became lopsided.

Gary believes that the institute, with little improvement over the years, is Teach For America's critical flaw. He points out that in scrapping the old model, the institute lost its greatest strengths.

> The institute needs to be a combination of Teach For America alum, who provide the realistic view, and diverse experts from all over the country, who provide the how-to. Teach For America's slowness to

change, particularly regarding improving the institute, is what hurts them the most.

After completing their own two-year commitments, hundreds of Teach For America alumni return to the institute, this time in leadership positions. They serve as Corps Member Advisors, Faculty Advisors, Workshop Presenters, Curriculum Specialists, and School Directors. Whatever their titles, they share a common mission: to provide corps members with the best possible training. Often alums make the trek to institutes to improve on what they consider to be deficiencies in their own training. Melissa Dyckes Storm (1994, Southern Louisiana) came to the institute in 2000, 2001, and 2002 as a Curriculum Specialist:

> I went back to the institute because my own experience had so miserably prepared me that I didn't want anyone else to be that poorly prepared. The improvement has been astronomical. Now there's a clearly mapped-out curriculum. The trainers, people like me, have been through the Teach For America experience. We send corps members out every day to teach in summer schools. They work with students who closely mirror the populations they'll be serving in their own sites. There is a huge amount of responsibility and accountability for corps members.

Alan Giuliani's (1994, Mississippi Delta) position as a Corps Member Advisor at the 1999 institute talked about how the institute had improved:

> Teach For America is far better in training corps members about lesson planning and long-term planning. Whereas there was no accountability at my own institute, now corps members are measuring their students' achievements as well as raising the bar for high expectations.

Sarah Fang (1996, Phoenix) worked as a CMA from 1997–1999 because "I had a lot of struggles in my first year. I wanted to help the incoming corps avoid what I faced. I wanted to give them tools that I had to help them deal with the curriculum." Despite his ongoing critique of Teach For America, Gary Rubinstein has continued to stay involved with the institute even as he created his own 1991 workshop. He returns to Houston and New York each year to lead workshops about classroom management. Gary Rubinstein has continued to stay involved with workshops since his own 1991 institute.

> I created this workshop to fill the gaps of the institute. My first year was a disaster. No one told me how hard it was going to be. I go back to the institute every year to send the incoming corps that exact message—how hard it will be.

With regard to his workshop, Gary explained the following:

> Corps members love the workshop, and attendance is often about one hundred people, though the average TFA workshop draws only about fifteen participants. Corps members have said things like, "I learned more in this one hour than I did in the whole institute." I take statements like that as a compliment, but they are also disturbing since it means the institute is not improving enough.

Gary sees the irony of the situation that Teach For America does not invite him to the institute. "Even though many corps members have said it was the more useful hour of the institute, when I go to Houston, I pay my own airfare."

Creating the most effective institute means preparing corps members for the challenges their students will face. Melissa Dyckes Storm reveals that there is work to be done in regard to training its special education teachers:

> My concern now with the institute is their focus on special education. It's not really an institute-wide focus. There are workshops on working with children with special needs. Corps members are placed at two

summer schools that serve special education students, but not everyone has immediate contact with special education students.

Melissa pointed out that that problem is twofold:

> First it sets up this awkward dynamic between corps members, sort of like "They're working with those kids." Second, we all need to be equipped to serve these students. Realistically, there are students with special needs in every classroom across the country, whether or not they've been recognized and diagnosed.

Before corps members scatter across the region, they come together on the last night of the institute to reflect about the lessons learned, the work yet to be done, and the importance of their efforts. Matthew Schmitt (1999, New Orleans) delivered the following speech, "The Value of Spirals," at the 1999 institute closing ceremony:

> I noticed, as I was lecturing about metaphor and simile to my ninth-grade English class at Davis High School in Houston, that one of my students [Mary] in the front row was doodling in her notebook. I paused, as I had just posed a question. I looked over at what she was doodling. She was creating spirals. Starting at a center and winding out and out. There were about a dozen of them around the page. For me, it was becoming a trance.
>
> Looking back, I see the value of those spirals. I had always believed in the circle, the way it is all-inclusive, the way you can rely on it to always come back to where it starts. But a circle is stagnant. It doesn't take you anywhere, unless it's a wheel. On the other hand, a spiral has a direction, not as definite and efficient as a straight line, but it indeed makes progress away from where it begins. My path as a teacher is becoming a spiral, one that is frustratingly slow-moving, one that has the potential to make me very dizzy, but one that allows me to be close to where I've come from, and to not go back. Every failure and success along the way is visible; for the spiral draws vision inwards as it moves

outwards. I look back towards the center as I move with new directions. For the first time in my life, every single belief is being tested. Here at the institute, our belief is high expectations, and summer school has been our proving ground. Here, I see my idealism and reality begin to spin around each other like a ying-yang.

My first lesson was to teach one of my favorite poems. It was a poem that I studied in college, and keeping with our belief of high expectations, I felt that our students could appreciate and understand its powerful message. The poem is called "St. Francis and the Sow" by Galway Kinnell. It is about the beauty of a mother pig, and it draws a complex picture of her sadly down in the mud, among the slops, yet all the while nursing her fourteen babies. I felt strangely connected to this sow. The mud that I was in was my own self-doubt, my own exhaustion, my own lack of inspiration for a lesson plan. The way I asked myself too many times, "Did TFA make a mistake with me? How is it that I'm here?"

My head started to spin as I looked up at the blank stares in my classroom. Then Kassandra quietly said, "Mr. Schmitt, I think people can be like flowers. They are beautiful and they can blossom." And I said, "You've got it, Kassandra." Because the heart of the poem is about how everything blossoms. Even a sow who lives in the mud. Even a teacher who feels lost. The idea is that, when we are feeling low, we tend to lose sight of our importance, and need to be reminded. The institute had brought out every facet of my personality, but I was too often depressed at how it drudged up my low and ugly sides. I'm remembering through this poem, through Kassandra's comments, that my hard work, my dedication, despite the mud, and my love for this endeavor is, indeed, beautiful. And even though my lesson failed at producing the stimulating discussion I had envisioned, it did allow for a few subtle miracles to occur. Kassandra's comment kept me going, gave me enough energy to keep spinning.

A spiral. The forward progress I was making suddenly turned back the other way. But I'm learning slowly, and I am so thankful that our students were willing to teach me also. Reflecting back, looking deep inside, growing outwardly with hope and new knowledge.

Now, this is my final lesson here in Houston. The objective: Students will be able to remember the lovely and beautiful reasons that they wanted to become teachers.

Will everyone please close your eyes with me? Please think back to the first time you heard about Teach For America. Think about your initial impressions, how you struggled with all the other options you considered before making this commitment. Think about those salient reasons you chose to teach. Hold those reasons, hold on to them dearly, and after holding for a few seconds, open your eyes.

Imagine your reasons harmonizing with the teacher's next to you, and everyone's in this room. In your own spiraled progressions through this complicated world of public education, remember that you are beautiful and you are making an important difference. Remember to use the force. Remember to learn from your student's doodling. For Mary's spirals give me hope, because if we were all to leave Houston in a straight line, we might never connect again. But in spirals we will spin into each other often, and the patterns of our paths will create a framework as delicate and lovely as fine lace, as intricate as a New Orleans jazz quartet, but as strong as the nets under acrobats. So flip and twist and spin above the crowd and hang on to that bar.

Spirals like a creative tornado, not a destructive one, but one that inspires students to fly above rainbows. And never forget to look inwards as you radiate outwards. Never forget to remember.

After five weeks of trial runs in the summer school, corps members take the responsibility of seeking out additional training and support to carry them through their two years. Teach For America makes no claims that corps members will be fully prepared after only five weeks for their placements. Corps Member Advisors, Literacy Consultants, and School Directors urge new teachers to continue in their own education, to enroll in credentialing classes, and to actively seek out answers to their questions about classroom management, long-term planning, and reading assessment. With heads spinning from information overload, corps members gather a plethora of precious guidance. They are told to be earnest in their communities and in their schools. They are reminded that teaching will be a struggle, but advised to rely on parents, administrators, fellow teachers, and Teach For America alumni for support and guidance. Corps members are encouraged to stay active with the national Teach For America movement and to keep a sense of perspective.

And so corps members gather up chalk, write their first lesson plans, and disperse across the nation to their prospective regions. In the youthful passion and inspiring talk at the summer institute, the realities of full-time teaching seem far away. Some corps members may feel unprepared, others may feel confident in their new teacher personas, but most are surprised by the challenges that begin the very second when they stand in the front of a classroom and introduce themselves to their new students as their teacher.

The summer institute is the best that Teach For America can do, but it's not enough. I don't know if there's ever enough time and training to prepare you for the challenges ahead.

—Aaron Amitin (2001, New York)

chapter four

raw realities

The hurdles that a Teach For America teacher faces are innumerable: outdated or non-existent textbooks, unequipped science labs, and students who come to class tired and malnourished.
— Brent Maddin (1999, Southern Louisiana) in a speech for the 2001 Teach For America summer institute

Teach For America corps members venture into schools with massive teacher turnover, overcrowding, and minimal resources. They accept the placements that are turned down by veteran teachers. Though he barely spoke Spanish, David Silver (1995, Los Angeles) filled a vacant classroom teaching third grade bilingual. Angela Franks (2000, North Carolina) taught behaviorally and emotionally disabled middle school students. Katherine Onorato (1999, Oakland) was sent to a notoriously rough middle school in East Oakland, where classrooms went empty year-round. Melinda Manning (1994, Mississippi Delta) taught in a classroom where rats and snakes crawled over students' feet. Kate Driscoll (1998, Washington, D.C.) taught in a custodian's closet. Marion Johnson (2001, New Mexico) witnessed the bleak realities of isolation, alcoholism, and poverty in the Navajo Nation. Here corps members comment on the obstacles of public education: realities for teachers, realities for students, and realities of public schools.

> *The realities of public schools are this: Kids go to school hungry, kids go to school scared, kids go to school without getting the attention they need at home.*
>
> —Benjamin Rayer (1991, Los Angeles)

the hardest jobs

Because teaching positions are assigned on archaic rules of seniority, the least-prepared teachers are assigned the toughest classrooms. This system often puts Teach For America teachers in the most difficult placements—in special education classes, bilingual classes, and limited-English classes.

David Silver (1992, Los Angeles) recalled being "really scared" by his second grade bilingual placement at a Compton elementary school:

> The last Spanish I had taken was in high school. I scored a 1 (out of 5) on the Spanish Advanced Placement exam. But even that placement showed me the reality of the situation; the reality was that I was the most qualified person to fill that position. I spoke the most Spanish of any other candidate, despite the fact that I spoke virtually no Spanish. Though I was certainly not bilingual, and maybe totally unqualified to teach that position, there was a desperate need for teachers. This school district was grabbing at straws to fill classrooms.

Allison Greenwood (2000, New Orleans) taught in at a high school in Louisiana's New Orleans parish, where disengaged students, absenteeism, and truancy were immediate obstacles. Allison explained that because of pervasive absenteeism and truancy, there were no reliable counts of enrolled students:

I would have forty or fifty kids on a roster, but it was rare for more than twenty-six to show up for class. I spent a ton of time sending letters home and phoning parents to figure out which kids were actually in my class.

When addresses were incorrect and phone numbers disconnected, students were simply unaccounted for. Resources were scarce. In her first year, Allison went without science textbooks and computers. The school climate impeded instruction: "Sometimes the hallways were so loud that it was nearly impossible to teach."

With these challenges, Allison found meaningful ways to reach and engage her students:

First you have to establish respect. It takes a lot of effort, creativity, and pain. You must be firm and confident in what you're doing. I can't always speak about raising my students' test scores, but I do know that 70% of my students attend my class three to four times a week, which is more than the school average. Some of my tenth graders read their first book ever in my classroom and wrote four-page essays about it with a thesis and footnotes. I judge their growth on their ability to read, be engaged in, and discuss novels.

There's no job more difficult than teaching special education.
—Matthew Lenaghan (1993, Houston)

Tough jobs often mean tough classes, as in the case of Mina Kim (1998, New Jersey). As a rookie teacher, Mina was assigned to a challenging first grade classroom:

The veteran teachers had gotten together and hand-selected their rosters. The leftover students were filtered to my classroom. I got a class with tremendous needs. One-half of my students had documented special needs, some with severe ADHD and others with dark and violent tendencies. On the second day, a teacher walked by my students in the hallway. She looked at me and said, "I guess you're the new special education teacher."

Angela Franks (2000, North Carolina) was placed in a self-contained special education classroom, serving middle school students with disabilities from severe emotional problems to psychiatric disorders. The impending obstacles did not scare Angela, who was "so excited to take on such an amazing challenge." In fact, she recalled "begging and pleading" to keep her placement when the Teach For America regional office considered switching her to an alternative vacancy.

Rather than being in mainstream classrooms, Angela's students spend the day with a smaller number of students and instruction modified to address their academic needs. Angela immediately noticed the divide between her students and the mainstream population. "Mainstream students come to school, eat breakfast, and hang out in the gym. My students stay on school buses while the rest of the student body eats breakfast. Everyone knows who my students are." Angela's goal was to help her students feel normal, build their self-esteem, and show them their capabilities and ways to be successful. Angela explained, "I am always trying new ways to invest my students in their own futures and education." She worked with students to set new goals for every class period and in the process, became emotionally invested:

> I know my students on a personal level, their histories, their families. I'm very real with them. They know that I'm their teacher, but I'm their number one advocate. I am the first person to tell them that they've done something right and the first to tell them they've done something wrong. I am the closest thing to a mother that they'll have in school. Trust is the key to our personal relationships, and from that mutual respect everything works much better.

With these huge challenges came daily frustrations. "We will make huge progress, and then we'll go backwards." The 2002–2003 school year marked Angela's third year in her original placement. She stayed because "I didn't feel ready to leave. The amount I could do in an extra year is amazing." Her devotion to her students and her tireless efforts have already translated to measurable success. By the end of her second year, two of her students fully exited the school's special education program, with another four spending half the day in mainstream classes and the other half in Angela's classroom:

> Before, I would get phone calls during the day from mainstream teachers to come get my students out of their classes. Now mainstream teachers have stopped me in the hallway to praise my students. Some students have undergone a 180-degree turnaround.

When reflecting on her Teach For America experience, Angela concluded, "This experience isn't about me. I'm doing this to make an impact on my kids. I need constantly to focus on what I can do to help my kids. It's not an opportunity to show how successful or amazing individual teachers are, but rather how successful and amazing our students are." Future plans for Angela include earning a master's in fine arts, teaching college photography, and possibly working on educational policy.

in the hardest schools

In Katherine Onorato's (1999, Bay Area) experience, the hardest schools could not attract and keep teachers. On October 31, 2000, the cover story of the *San Francisco Chronicle* focused on Katherine's East Oakland middle school, stating that its poor conditions and low achievement deemed state intervention necessary:

> The state has given it three years to improve or face strict sanctions, including the possibility of being shut down. . . . It has the second-highest suspension rate in Oakland. Students come and go so often that no one is certain who is enrolled. Experienced teachers are hard to attract and keep.

The state of California measures progress in public schools by how much each school improves on the state's Academic Performance Index, a scale of two hundred to one thousand points based primarily on test scores and student achievement. A score of eight hundred is considered excellent. Katherine's school scored 440 points. The school was given one year to improve its API score to 458 points to avoid a state takeover. Katherine's first year was a mix of "panic and anger." The most pressing obstacle came in filling classrooms:

> It was disheartening—this constant need for teachers. The staff turnover at my school in one year was 50%—and that was amongst a staff of twenty-five. There were three or four classrooms that were just revolving doors. One teacher would go in, quit, and be out—over and over again. To be fair, one of the teachers who quit was TFA 1999. These kids, so many of whom had little or no stability at home, also had no stability at school. Kids would learn to scare teachers out of positions or just give up entirely, since they suspected their teacher wouldn't make it through the year. When I arrived, my kids bragged about how many teachers they had run off. When I told them I was here to stay, their response was "Yeah, right" and "You'll be going soon."

The high turnover reaped ill effects on students and teachers:

> There seemed to be no school community. You can't build a community amongst the teachers when there is so much turnover. As a teacher, it was hard to support my fellow teachers with this suspicion that they would leave. There was huge burnout among the teachers that did stay since we were covering tough classrooms, covering vacancies during our periods off, and trying to support new teachers in hopes that they would stay.

Tough schools also translate into bleak environments and negative school climates:

There was this depressing aura about the school—beyond its destroyed buildings, beyond the poverty of the neighborhood. There was this sense of hopelessness that pervaded the school, this feeling that there was no way to get out of the situation. The kids spent so much time being angry about external forces that they weren't able to focus on their abilities. They develop this sense of defensiveness. They became hardened by poverty and violence, and their parents didn't think they were scared of anything since they have seen it all. They had so few role models. Their parents, cousins, uncles were in jail. It felt like too many kids had checked out, too many kids had already given up.

Michael Siegel (1999, Bay Area) explained the impact that poor resources had on his students:

In Oakland, there are a handful of wretched schools. There are schools where people are forgotten. It was like the end of the world down there [in East Oakland]. There was no playground equipment, no recess supervision. The kids had recess on cracked asphalt. They would throw rocks at each other. There was no art, no music.

Michael was so frustrated by the poor shape of his school that he delivered the following speech to the Oakland School Board on June 28, 2001:

Take the layout of the school: twelve hundred students in grades K–5, spread over a campus originally designed for five hundred. The upper yard that I inhabit with my nineteen third grade students used to be a playing field and park for the community, but now is covered with broken asphalt and fourteen portable classrooms. My room, portable #57, has been there for fifty-five years. During the day, the kids scramble around the buildings in games of hide-and-seek and football, but after hours the corridors between the rooms serve as a hideaway for anyone that needs it. I often find broken bottles, empty blunt cigar casings, used condoms, and other trash when I come to school in the morning.

After school, when I stay to pack boxes or sort curricula, there are groups of teens sitting on my porch who seem surprised when I return from the copy room; and there remains the graffiti, the empty dime bags, and the evidence of teen indulgence when I have left. Every once in a while, they break into the classrooms themselves.

Equally exasperating was Michael's realization that his school failed to provide services for students who needed individualized attention or intervention. He recalled how the realities of public schools impacted two of his second graders, Tevin, in need of counseling intervention, and Louis, in need of special education instruction:

Tevin was a special education student who was emotionally disturbed. He was supposed to be receiving services for his emotional and academic needs, but in reality he received very little. The counseling program seemed to be a half-baked intervention that wasn't followed through. Tevin would come to school and tell me stories of how he spent his evenings running around the city, even running through the tunnels of storm drains. Tevin came to my classroom with a file from Child Protective Services. He was abused by his alcoholic father. His grandfather had been lynched in the 1960s by the Ku Klux Klan. He would throw rocks at other kids on the playground. His behavior problems stemmed from a childhood of abuse, poverty, neglect. Tevin made me realize that the worst kids have the worst stories. There's a reason for everything—behavior, attitudes, academic performance. Unfortunately, I realized too often that these reasons were often economically based.

Louis lived in a house where his parents worked seven days a week. He had three other brothers, the oldest being fifteen. Basically with the parents gone all the time, the boys ran the house. Louis acted like a thug in school. He ran wild on the playground, hit other kids, and was incapable of controlling his anger. Moreover, Louis had a learning disability and received one hour of specialized instruction in a special education day class. So this kid, who needed serious academic intervention as well as behavior modification, was getting one hour a day to specifically address his needs. It was laughable. It was easy to look at a kid like Louis, who needed so much personal attention, and see how kids slip through the cracks of public education.

David Silver (1995, Los Angeles) offered the example of his second grade student Raoul to show the other extreme of students not getting the services they needed:

> Raoul was the smartest second grader I've ever met. He was totally on the mark in everything—light-years ahead in reading, math, writing. He scored in the 98th percentile on his standardized tests. I wanted to challenge him, so I got some advanced-level materials—books, stories which I thought would really challenge him. I remember bringing him the chapter book *Frog and Toad Are Friends*. I later discovered that this book was benchmarked at a high first grade reading level. It was a total disservice to Raoul and holding him back, hurting his ability.
>
> I tried for a month to get Raoul into a GATE program—Gifted and Talented. It was an organizational nightmare getting through the paperwork of the referral process and trying to find out who the GATE coordinator was. I finally found out that there wasn't really a GATE program, no real services for kids who were achieving at the high-end of the spectrum. Three years later, I found out that Raoul had changed schools. His family had moved just so Raoul could attend school in a neighboring district, one that could better serve him with better resources and better programs. It seemed to me to be this indication that schools were doing a disservice to kids of so many levels. When it comes to public education and resources, we usually assume it's the special education students who are lacking. But what about the students at the other extreme—the Raouls who are being limited in their achievement because of poor resources?

Rebecca Travers (1998, Houston) taught at a school so chaotic that teachers and students alike came to regard it as "the toughest school in Houston." With that label came a sense of pride among students and staff, as they worked together to defy the odds. Not only could the school not retain teachers, but there was also administrative turnover as well—with principals and assistant principals leaving each year. Although Rebecca came to regard her experience with Teach For America as "phenomenal," she quickly faced frustrations with the school and the school district:

> In my Teach For America interview, I remember being asked "What would you do if on the first day of school, fifty kids showed up for your class?" I told my interviewer that I would send a student to the office to get more desks. My interviewer responded that there were no more desks or chairs—then what? I answered that I would take the class to the gym and we'd have class in the gym. My interviewer told me that the gym was locked—now what? I finally answered that I would just cram all the kids in my classroom, they'd have to stand and deal with it. At the time I remember thinking what a random question. But on my first day of school, it made sense. In some classes, I had fifty-five kids in each class for the first two weeks of school. There was no sense of urgency to resolve the situation and it was frustrating to see how slowly the overcrowding got resolved.

Though her classes were eventually reduced, she still taught from thirty to forty students per class. In addition to the overcrowding, Rebecca pointed out the abysmal resources of the school:

> The school itself was filthy, because custodians were so understaffed. The week before classes started I went into school to get my classroom ready. I remember cleaning roaches out of desks. It was such a dirty facility that it caused health problems for students and teachers. In terms of resources, my initial budgetary allotment lasted me two months. After that, there was nothing. Most of the supplies that we needed—things for labs, paper, pencils—I bought out of my own pocket. You were lucky if the Xerox machine worked. Most of the time it didn't. We had no textbooks. The ones we had were more than five

years old, they didn't correlate with the curriculum, and there weren't enough for students to take home with them.

An ineffective administration contributed to a chaotic school climate:

> The school was not effective at all in providing any sort of structures.
> In the case of behavior problems, the administration did nothing to
> help with discipline. Teachers were not permitted to send a student to
> the office without first contacting the parent. In my classroom, if two
> students started fighting, I couldn't send them out without calling
> home. So I would try to call home and find out that the student didn't
> have a working home phone, or that the student's mother worked the
> night shift and wouldn't get off work until two in the morning. As a
> first-year teacher, I sent two kids to the office who were fighting, and
> they were sent straight back to me with a note from the assistant princi-
> pal that I needed to contact home first. It was ridiculous.

Teachers were hard to come by. Over 50% of teachers were uncertified and substitute teachers were nearly impossible to get. When teachers were absent, their classes were divided up and sent to other classrooms. "There were some days that I had my forty kids plus another twenty kids from another classroom where the teacher was absent." Rebecca dismissed any thoughts that the school was depressing:

> The kids had no self-pity. My students relied on their sense of humor
> and their wisdom to pull through the struggles. There were noble vet-
> eran teachers who had grown up in the area and stayed for thirty years.
> My kids always showed an enormous appetite to learn and they were
> hysterically funny. As an individual, I tried to raise the standard to chal-
> lenge them and to give them effective and applicable academic and life
> lessons.

Rebecca concluded that the disorganization of her school was "shameful."

These kids weren't having their basic needs met at home. School was supposed to be their haven from that—but really it was just as chaotic as their homes. There was no safety, no security, no clear expectations for them at school.

in the hardest districts

Schools fell upon neighborhood lines. Rich neighborhoods mean rich schools. We, as Teach For America corps members, are sent into the poor neighborhoods. Poor neighborhoods mean poor schools.
—Rebecca Travers (1998, Houston)

In 2001, Marion Johnson was one of twenty-three pioneer Teach For America corps members who were placed in New Mexico's Navajo Nation. The Navajo Nation has a long history of educational trouble and a wide range of social problems, including poverty, alcoholism, and abuse. Upon the removal of Native Americans by the federal government, Native Americans were forced into federal schools. Much of the purpose of these schools was to "Americanize" the Native Americans; they were not allowed to wear traditional dress nor talk in the Navajo language. Marion's placement brought a unique set of realities: students who lived without running water and electricity, the closest library being fifty-five miles away, and an average per capita income of $4,500:

The first challenge was recognizing that the Navajo Nation truly is a different culture bound by a different language and different beliefs. The reservation is a sovereign land, and with that sovereignty comes a whole new set of cultural differences. Much of my initial challenge was culture shock. I didn't understand what it meant to be living on a reservation, the isolation that it entailed, the difference in cultural interactions.

Marion taught a combination class of second and third graders, eighteen students total ranging in ages from six to nine. Her school was run by the Bureau of Indian Affairs, serving 160 Navajo students with only eight teachers. Of those eight teachers, only one was Navajo. The only other Navajos on staff were cafeteria workers, bus drivers, or teacher's aides. Since non-natives cannot own property on the reservation, Marion lived in a "teacherage"—a school-managed home provided to staff.

> There is huge mistrust in how children are being taught and how children are being treated. There is a quiet resentment on the reservation for people who come—teachers, doctors, service providers—and stay for only a year. You really have to prove yourself and your motivations. You have to prove that you are there for the right reasons—to teach these children, not that your mission is to save these children.

Marion pointed to the language barrier as another troublesome reality:

> My students were learning English and Navajo. Most of them only speak Navajo at home, so there is no language reinforcement, no carry-over of skills from classroom to home. Most of their parents only had high-school English skills. Three of my students lived with their grandparents, who only spoke Navajo. Not only did this hinder their skill level, but it also translated into a sort of identity crisis.

Marion's students also faced unique home problems.

> Poverty was a real issue. Alcoholism was a real issue. Abuse was a real issue. But my students, at the ages of seven or eight, had household responsibilities that were crucial to family survival. Students came to me telling me that they didn't do their homework because they were herding sheep, or chopping wood. If they didn't help with these jobs, they would go without something at home—a meal, or income. It was relatively common for kids to leave your classroom for four weeks, and

then return. Kids would move when their families were trying to find migrant work or there was a custody battle. As a teacher, I had to worry about issues of hygiene. Some of my kids lived without running water or electricity. The school gave students showers twice a week. I can't imagine a teacher in Compton or New York having to deal with shower time at school.

Marion also pointed to the isolation that pervaded every sense of life in the Navajo Nation—geographic, cultural, and social isolation:

> My students had no sense of the world outside the reservation, outside of the Southwest. Television was their only outlet. I remember reading my students a fairy tale the first week of school. They had no idea what a castle was. Things like that make you think about cultural awareness.

According to Marion, the isolation translated to a lack of services. "Families often don't know about what is available to them. They don't know to pick up the phone and call an abuse hotline or how to secure the services that are available for their children." Marion believed that this isolation limited future opportunities for her students. Though there was a middle school, high school, and even a junior college on the reservation, Marion wondered about the future possibilities for her children. "There are such strong ties to the family and the land that I wondered how my kids will meld into society. Will they stay on the reservation? Will they leave?"

Marion found teaching to be "very difficult. My standards—things like attendance and the quality of student work—were challenged early on." Marion also felt the strain of tight budgets and limited resources:

> Because we were controlled by the BIA (Bureau of Indian Affairs), the resources were scarce and there was a huge misuse of money. We didn't get textbooks until late October. The resources for science and math were particularly bad.

In fact, teachers were responsible for controlling the school's budget, which was reviewed at each monthly staff meeting. "I never thought that I, as a first-year teacher, would be responsible for budget decisions."

According to alum Morty Ballen (1992, Southern Louisiana), nowhere is the educational crisis more apparent than in Louisiana. With its long history of racial tension and poverty, Louisiana ranks at the bottom of the nation in terms of overall quality of life for children. Poverty hits hard in rural parishes where there is little industry. Forty-five of every one hundred public school freshmen do not graduate from high school. 90% of students qualify for reduced price or free lunches. The per-capita income is $13,190.

As a tenth grade English teacher, Morty Ballen had one student who was only twelve months younger than him. "He had failed so many times." For Morty, the toughest reality of Southern Louisiana was the "defacto segregation—Baton Rouge felt like a depressed Southern town with strong racial legacies." Morty recalled being "enraged" at the "unjust social-political realities."

> Here I was, young and idealistic, having just joined an organization founded on the premise that all children—regardless of race, ethnicity, socioeconomic background—can learn. I came to Baton Rouge and faced this huge obstacle, teachers who were supposed to be my colleagues, who believed in the "black kids can't learn" notion. I can recall many racist jokes and comments being made in the teachers' lounge. I didn't challenge them, but I just left the teacher's lounge. I didn't want to be there. I have such vivid memories of walking out of the teachers' lounge at lunch in disbelief. This racism made me so angry. I felt I had this proof that the rights of these kids to attain an excellent education was being usurped.

Morty was discouraged "that there was so much injustice in poor areas, that kids were expected to fail, based on their race, before they entered the classroom." From his experience, he concluded that "schools simply aren't working." He blamed much of the failure of public schools on negative school environments, "where teachers are not expecting the best from their students. Too many times we are basing our educational assumptions on cultural views."

These testimonials paint a portrait of the realities that corps members face, the realities that seem to prohibit student learning and the realities that may discourage starry-eyed young teachers. Their work has just begun, and already the task feels insurmountable.

And time and time again, corps members rise to the challenge and figure out how to promote learning, how to inspire their students, and how to survive as a rookie teacher.

chapter five

initial impressions

I didn't have the first inkling of where to begin.
—Danielle DeLancey (2002, North Carolina)

With Teach For America, you take the worst of the worst and you make the best out of it.
—Susannah Nichols (2002, Detroit)

Teach For America corps members are expected to transcend the realities of public education to promote meaningful student learning. But with that challenge comes a wide array of sentiments, including self-doubt, disconnect, and disbelief. Corps members face a constant battle to keep their spirits up and to remember the commitment they have made as the realities of public schools leave many disappointed, overwhelmed, and defeated in the first months of teaching.

disbelief

There is such injustice in low-income areas. I couldn't help but think, "This is America and we still have kids that come to school without shoes."

—Bill Norbert (1991, New Orleans)

My first impressions were that there was a lot of sadness, a lot of pain, and a lot of unmet needs in low-income neighborhoods.

—Mina Kim (1998, New Jersey)

Many corps members have come to Teach For America hopeful that they will make a difference, but disillusionment strikes when they face the impeding obstacles. In 2002, Teach For America brought forty corps members to Detroit, including Alissa Naymark (2002, Detroit). Detroit Public Schools, which serve 167,000 students, face serious inequity. In 2000, only about one-third of the district's students scored at grade level on the Metropolitan Achievement Test of reading, math, and science. In 1999, only 22% of the district's fourth graders and 33% of seventh graders demonstrated satisfactory or proficient reading competencies on the Michigan Educational Assessment program. The state of Michigan presents many barriers in the teacher certification process, and thus corps members are not state-certified upon completing their commitments. Moreover, corps members teach as Extended Substitutes in regular positions, which gives them less job security and lower pay.

Alissa was shocked to find students hostile to education and a culture of fear and subordination. Students demonstrated their bitterness by refusing to do work.

There wasn't a love of learning generated by my school or the larger system. It wasn't as if students walk quietly in the hallway to not disturb the classes that are learning, but more because of the consequences of the mean security guard yelling at them.

Charter corps member Sarah Van Orman (1990, Rural Georgia) underwent "complete culture shock" on her transition. Her disbelief pertained to the racial divide of her placement. Of eight hundred students, 99% were African American, 80–90% of the staff was African American, and Sarah, as a young white woman, was absolutely the minority. The lack of resources and ineffective teaching led to the realization that, "We had brilliant students that received such a poor education. The legacy of racism and poverty denies opportunities for even bright, motivated students who want to succeed." Melissa Dyckes Storm (1994, Southern Louisiana) echoed the presence of institutional racism brought by the rural poverty of St. John's Parish in Southern Louisiana. "There were clear lines of segregation drawn. White teachers chose to eat in their own lunchroom. I heard countless comments of "those dumb black kids who can't learn."

isolation

First impressions for many corps members—primarily those in rural placements—are inextricably linked to the geographic, social, cultural, and academic isolation of their regions. For Anne Sung (2000, Rio Grande Valley), the geographic isolation of South Texas meant that academic resources, like libraries and bookstores, were almost nonexistent. Immediately Murray Carlisle (1997, Mississippi Delta) noted, "The Delta felt hot, flat, desolate. It was isolating. It was closed off and felt resistant to change. Everything else felt another world away." Caitlin Wittig (1997, Rio Grande Valley) witnessed how geographic isolation leads to limited academic opportunities:

> It felt like there was this recycled knowledge in the Valley. There were lots of smart innovative people, but because no one left there was no new influx of ideas. There are no new tools to expand what goes on.

disconnect

> *It's not true that all Teach For America corps members are welcomed*
> *with open arms into communities. I was respected, but there was an*
> *initial circumspect about who I was and why I was there.*
> —Molly Blank (1998, Washington, D.C.)

Corps members face an enormous transition integrating themselves into new communities, where they are sometimes perceived as outsiders. Race and ethnicity complicate community integration. Melinda Manning (1994, Mississippi Delta) worried about how she, as a young white woman, would be perceived in the South: "I felt like I was in a different country. It was the first time in my life where I was the only white person. Other teachers seemed suspicious of me." Racial identity presents similar challenges to corps members who identify themselves as people of color. Nakia Whitney (1996, New Jersey) explained, "In my school, all of the teachers were white. I stood out because I was black. I didn't want to stand out even more because of my TFA label, so I kept it to myself." Mina Kim (1998, New Jersey) sensed that her students' parents were initially wary of her, as a young Asian-American woman. "The more I worked to contact their parents, the less my ethnicity became an issue." Bill Murphy (2000, New Orleans) understood the delicate nature of community integration:

> I was very conscious that my presence in an entirely African-American community might be interpreted with the "white knight" message. But we, as corps members, must keep in mind that we are not in these schools to save anybody. I never said that I was a part of a movement to save people. I was in New Orleans because there was a classroom that might be empty without me.

Murray Carlisle (1997, Mississippi Delta) was respectful in his new community. "I was naturally curious about other cultures and I wasn't condescending or patronizing." Angela Franks (2000, North Carolina) echoed the value of humility:

> I went to my region knowing that I was a guest here. I was the visitor. I thanked people for letting me be here. I tried to show people that I was interested in getting to know them. I didn't want people to mystify who I was or where I was from.

Nancy Taylor (1999, Rio Grande Valley) spoke about her efforts to integrate herself into the relative seclusion of the Rio Grande Valley:

> As a newcomer to the community, I was always reaching out to others—teachers, parents, community leaders. I came to have the utmost respect for veteran teachers that had served before me. I didn't rank people, I didn't judge people. There's nothing phenomenal about this— but as newcomers, we need to be sensitive to the people who grow up in these communities, to the people who spend their lives working towards change here. We need to treat human beings like human beings. As a result, I feel like I became a part of the community and the community became a part of me.

In the following piece, Nancy writes about how community acceptance is tied to humility, respect, and deference to those who have devoted their lives to community development. In it, she refers to her most important classroom goal: to develop a strong sense of community in which students worked together to get to a better place. Nancy encouraged students to work "*con ganas*"—with great desire or heart. Nancy looked back at the entire community and came to understand the degree to which they all worked con ganas:

> These are the stories of the Rio Grande Valley, the stories of my students, my fellow teachers, the community. I want to tell these stories, because they all worked con ganas. Mayra—an easily distracted student who was not usually willing to sit still or bother herself with learning.

In my second year, we forged a strong relationship, a bond that kept her coming in voluntarily to tutoring sessions. She came to confide in me personally about home problems. She also was the first and last one there for the community or outside school activities I sponsored. Mayra struggled in many classes, and especially on the standardized tests. The social studies test was one of the only tests she passed, and she passed it at the highest level. She sat there an extra couple of hours. What ganas. Abby and Corina—best friends, both trying to be better students, both with huge familiy responsibilities and difficult home lives. Both of them were the first ones ready to volunteer and help tutor students, package food, or any other community project we did. Helping con ganas. Arturo—still calling me and writing me all summer just to talk. Arturo was annoying many of the girls around school last year and I constantly was teaching my sixth graders about ways to deal with conflict. When another problem arose, he and another student came up to me to mediate so they could find a way to work together again. It was beautiful. Mrs. Padilla—teacher for almost ten years. The epitome of teacher— she wills those students to succeed. She had also been so influential and strong, a fair and balanced voice for change in our district. She is persistent, committed, and always has faith in others. She is my friend and role model in life. Cristal—a special education student that had a hard time with her peers and in classes. She had an extremely difficult home life with little support. But she kept up in all her classes. As March rolled around, she did all her homework, tutoring, everything possible. And she inspired all of us at the school. She had ganas. Mr. and Mrs. Borrego, reading specialists. They believe so strongly in all students, have persevered themselves and for their family, and relentlessly work to help students read and understand their world. Beyond ganas. These people are the people who have given me a home and a community.

After three years of teaching, Nancy Taylor left the Valley to pursue a Masters in Public Policy from Harvard University's School of Government. She plans to return to the Rio Grande Valley offering a new model of education leadership and community empowerment in the schools.

the struggle to survive

I was stepping into something where I didn't know the answers.
—Clare Pinchin (1999, Bay Area)

Almost immediately many corps members grapple with classroom management, rule enforcement, following through with consequences, and maintaining an environment to promote learning. The ability to control a room of fourth graders, seventh graders, or eleventh graders is often a young teacher's biggest obstacle. Melissa Dyckes Storm (1994, Southern Louisiana) came to the classroom with "zero management skills." She remembered her first year as "a living nightmare. I put on blinders as a means of survival. I didn't realize how bad it was. I knew I would go home so exhausted. I knew I would go home crying. Determination got me through that first year."

Gary Rubinstein (1991, Houston) concluded that his first year of teaching was a disaster because of his inability to maintain classroom management. In the following humorous essay, Gary writes about his daily behavior debacles. Similar stories can be found in Gary's book, *Reluctant Disciplinarian* (Cottonwood Press, 1999). He hopes his experience will prevent new teachers, particularly TFA teachers, from suffering through the kind of first year he had.

I began my first year with all the idealism and enthusiasm of the TFA summer institute. Between September and November, my outlook shifted from quixotic to chaotic. Melba, my TFA support director, explained discipline consequences like this: "The first level is to warn them by saying the student's name firmly. If the behavior continues, write the student's name on the board. Next, put a check next to the name and after that you can do many things: Time out in the back of the room, calling parents, detention.

"Alex!" He was at it again. For days, I had followed Melba's advice. Warning, board, check. Warning, board, check. While for some kids, saying their names firmly would silence them for the rest of the period, Alex would freeze only while I was saying his name. As I turned my head to continue the lesson, his head would turn simultaneously back toward the student who sat behind him, to resumé his conversation.

Originally I reserved a spot on the side of the board for writing names, but I soon tired of stopping and walking over there constantly. To save time, I started writing the names wherever I happened to be standing. As a result, names were randomly scrawled all over the board. When I needed more space for the math examples, I had to carefully erase around the names.

By the end of an average period, I had issued twenty warnings, written fifteen names on the board, punctuated twelve checks. In all, I'd stopped class forty-seven times in a fifty-minute period. My once boundless options, I felt, had been systematically reduced to three.

My first option was to "roll with it." I could accept that only five minutes of each hour would consist of learning, while the rest of the time would be dominated by me begging kids to be respectful of their classmates. At least I'd learn to be a better teacher for my second year. I didn't choose this option because the program I joined was called "Teach For America" and not "Learn How To Teach For America."

My second possibility was to quit. My inability to control my classes, I felt, was harming the kids by impeding them from learning math. My TFA friend Jon tried to persuade me to stay: "If you quit you'll be teaching them that when things get rough, the best thing to do is quit." I countered with "No. I'll be teaching them that if they get a good education, like I did, they won't have to work a job that makes them miserable." Though I fantasized about quitting, almost daily, I knew that I wouldn't. I would eventually find something that worked.

My mentor said if my entire class was out of control, I should stop and wait before continuing my lesson. I could even sit at my desk and open the newspaper to demonstrate how serious I was. Tactics like this may have been possible if it was the entire class, but it never was. There were always three or four kids that sat there quietly no matter what mayhem occurred around them. For those kids, I had to choose a less subtle option—one that would let those few kids in each class know that even though I was going down, at least I was going down fighting.

My third, and final, alternative was to resort to the only method that required no skill in teaching or classroom management—I screamed my head off. My first scream won me ten minutes of cooperation, in which I taught a very tight lesson on percents. As the novelty wore off, my screams became less effective, sometimes only gaining me a few minutes of silence, just enough to teach one more concept. And that's how I made it through my first year. Scream. Teach for two minutes. Repeat as needed.

Corps members in the Mississippi Delta face a unique challenge: corporal punishment, which is not only still legal, but is readily enforced in some schools as a crucial means to behavior management. Cindy Zmijewski-Demers (1993, Mississippi Delta) recalled feeling "sick to [her] stomach just hearing about corporal punishment." Melinda Manning (1994, Mississippi Delta) revealed its cultural norm; "Corporal punishment was something that was expected by the students, the parents, the community." Cindy concurred that "corporal punishment was so ingrained that students expected it, parents suggested it." These corps members face the individual decision of whether or not to enforce corporal punishment in their classrooms. Corps members who resisted might open the door for extreme management problems. Cindy explained, "Since they knew I wouldn't do it in my classroom, kids would save up their aggression for my classroom." Additionally, at a time when corps members are trying to integrate themselves into schools and communities, refusing to participate in corporal punishment may alienate them even further. Cindy revealed, "On some level, I think my resistance to do corporal punishment caused problems with other teachers and my principal. They saw me as a white Northerner who thought she knew better than their ways." In spite of her personal disdain for corporal punishment, Melinda Manning relied on it in extreme circumstances:

I felt like it was something I should do. At my school, it was an integral part of the behavior management system. I didn't rely on it much, but my kids knew that when push came to shove, I would do it. You have to adapt in order to survive. You do things that you normally wouldn't do.

the enormity of the job

Many corps members are struck with the personal and professional enormity of the job. Allison Serafin (2001, Houston) felt an overwhelming responsibility:

My kids needed so much more than I could provide. They needed a big sister, a social worker, a private tutor, a mother. In my first year of teaching, I tried to play so many roles that I took on their burdens.

Danielle DeLancey (2002, North Carolina) felt overwhelmed by the needs of her students:

I teach one class where 50% of my students need major modifications for learning disabilities. Yet in that same class are several GATE [Gifted and Talented] students. I quickly realized that every child needs something, and it's totally overwhelming. I want to be able to give it to all of them.

Bill Murphy (2000, New Orleans) came to the classroom with the mentality that he was simply a teacher, approaching the job professionally and maintaining a personal distance. He quickly grew into a role much more profound:

I thought there would be a distance between my students and me, between the community and me. But you can't be just a teacher. Once the community decided I was trustworthy, once parents trusted me and treated me with respect, I became emotionally wrapped up.

The complexity of the teaching exceeds the personal realm and quickly applies to the professional, specifically the complexities of confusing policies, curriculums, and standards. Corps members point to great confusion and uncertainty regarding their first months in the classroom. Seth Morris (2001, Los Angeles) felt lost:

> My first goal was to figure out what to teach and how to teach. I didn't know what it meant to get students to grade level, or how to do that. It felt like I was given a classroom key, the state standards, and left on my own to figure it all out. My first year became about survival, day to day, week to week, and to the end of the year.

Right away, Jay Carney (1999, Baton Rouge) was overwhelmed and frustrated. "I felt lost in the woods. I wasn't comfortable with my persona in the classroom, which led to a sort of identity crisis." Much of his self-doubt came from his teaching assignment as a peer advisor. He was assigned a position as ninth grade "Peer Helper," teaching life and study skills, with a primary focus on gang-related violence, conflict resolution, and smoothing the academic transition from middle school to high school. He felt unqualified to teach in a position that lacked a concrete curriculum:

> I joined Teach For America to teach history, government, or some other social studies-related area, where I had a semblance of knowledge and experience. As a history teacher, Jay Carney had a reason and passion for teaching kids. As a Peer Helper, he did not. My lack of experience in counseling, relative youth, and the cultural differences with my students made me feel that I wasn't the right person for the job. I kept putting myself in the student's place. If I were in their shoes, would I have listened to me? It seemed patronizing for me to be telling them about how to solve their problems in the streets. I had no legitimacy as an instructor in my own eyes, and I didn't understand how to teach this course.

Even with his self-doubt, Jay continued to make his students his top priority:

I thought more about the welfare of my students than my own well-being. I left because my students deserved more than I could offer at the time. I was working 13–15 hour days, eating irregularly, and sleeping 4–5 hours a night. After a month of this, I was emotionally, physically, and mentally exhausted, and I finally just hit the wall. I checked myself into the doctor, took a few days off from school, and then decided to resign my position.

Jay Carney regretted not finishing his Teach For America commitment, but he looks at the experience as an ego-check and a turning point in his life. Though his decision to quit resulted from many personal circumstances, he does attribute some of his decision to the nature of Teach For America: "The lifestyle and habits which corps members learn at the institute are not necessarily sustainable; the expectations for immediate impact can be overwhelming." He is now a master's student in divinity at Duke University and keeps abreast of the challenges in teaching through his wife, a public school teacher in Durham, North Carolina.

am i the best thing for my kids?

The struggle to survive takes its emotional toll. Scott Joftus (1990, New York) felt guilt and self-doubt:

> I felt like I failed my first graders in the sense that I didn't really know how to teach them reading. It was hard to go home every day with that feeling—this nagging question of whether I was really doing more harm than good for my students.

Stephanie Crement (1999, Bay Area) became hypercritical:

> I got down on myself. There were days I felt I wasn't a good teacher, which quickly turned into me not being a good person. Struggling is such a part of the process, but my struggles and beliefs of my failure

ultimately made me be a better teacher. Through my own struggles, I could relate to how my kids felt when they struggled.

In my first year, I was always nagged by the hard questions of Am I really the best thing for my kids? Am I the best person to be doing what I'm doing? Am I as good as I would be if I were fully certified?

—Meghan Corman (2002, Los Angeles)

strength in numbers

I had family support, support from my school, and veteran teachers who took me under their wings. There was a whole community of people who supported me and my efforts. It felt like I would keep plugging away and they were there on the sidelines to help.

—Tom Shepley (1992, Baltimore)

Not all impressions are negative or heavy. Corps members are often pleasantly surprised by their welcome into communities and by the support that is available from a variety of sources. Guidance and mentoring comes from veteran teachers, supportive administrators, parents, and the Teach For America support network. Paul Holloman (1998, North Carolina) credited much of his smooth transition to his "phenomenal faculty. I stumbled through darkness for a bit, but they helped me find my bearings." Mina Kim (1998, New Jersey) worked under an administration that gave her autonomy and a vote of confidence:

My administration was very hands-off and I appreciated that. They trusted me immediately. It seemed as if they understood the realities of my challenges, but they were confident in my abilities.

Similarly Dennis Guikema (1994, Bay Area) benefited from the support of "outstanding principals who were real leaders and mentors." Moreover Dennis credited the parents of his students, who were a tremendous source of support:

> It was a two-sided beneficial relationship. On my side, I sought that support. On their side, they gave it to me. They were willing to give me that support while I learned.

Veteran teachers often take first-year corps members under their wings for mentoring, as in Anina Robb's case:

> Despite my training, I felt totally unprepared for the day-to-day realities of running a classroom. One of the things that got me through was my mentor. He was an older teacher who didn't teach my subject area or grade level—I taught middle school English, he was a music teacher. But he came to my classroom three days a week and told me how wonderful I was. Even if it wasn't true, it really helped to have an immediate positive response. He also gave me great tips for classroom procedures, how to set up and operate my classroom.

Support also comes from within the corps itself. Furman Brown (1990, Los Angeles) "survived because of the good teachers around me and the other corps members who saved my life."

love at first site

I loved my kids right from the start. My kids had a special kind of flavor, this character that I liked immediately.
—Scot Fishman (1997, Washington, D.C.)

Many corps members point out that their initial impressions are positive because of their well-functioning schools, their immediate affinity to their students, and communities that embrace education. Right from the start, Bill Norbert (1990, New Orleans) admired his students. "I fell in love with my kids. They were forced to grow up early. They had developed a tough exterior, but under that they were still so vulnerable." On a similar note, Lisa Leadbitter (1997, Houston) remarks, "My initial impressions were positive. I was prepared for this rough and tough situation. I was surprised by how cute and sweet my kids were." Cindy Zmijewski-Demers (1993, Mississippi Delta) discovered how eager her students were to learn. In an attempt to spend every minute on learning, the school eliminated physical education, music, art, and recess. Cindy believes that because the day was such drudgery, students "were so appreciative of critical thinking, creativity, and innovative teaching."

Finally, the most immediate realization corps members have pertains to the importance of reality in an organization which embraces idealism and preaches high expectations. Robin Gault (2001, Rio Grande Valley) believed she "left the idealism at the door, except for a few rare moments."

> My idealism is fairly fleeting, but I try to keep it in the back of my mind. My first year was all about realizing that I had a lot of learning, that I had to be the best I could possibly be all while surviving. My high expectations took a backseat to survival. I'm trying my best but I'm not closing the achievement gap. I'm more concerned with a really great lesson than the larger picture of getting students' reading levels up to the Teach For America expectations. I'm not concerned with the overall idealism.

chapter six

no magic recipe

I ate, slept, drank, and dreamt those kids. My students took over my life and my mindspace.

—Mina Kim (1998, New Jersey)

I always tell my students that as their teacher, I'm like a flashlight. I expose areas inside of them that were dark before. I'm not giving them anything new. I'm just shining on what they couldn't see before. I'm illuminating things inside of them to make them realize that they not only have the capabilities, but they can do anything with them.

—John Keisler (2000, New Jersey)

On a late August morning, the first day of school in Franklin, Louisiana, Sara Cotner (2000, Southern Louisiana) welcomed her class of third graders by telling them that they were the A+ class. "I have handpicked each and every one of you to be in my class," she explained. "I selected you because I knew you were smart and I knew you would work hard." The eyes of twenty third graders were on Sara as she instilled in students a strong belief in themselves.

A month later, Sara led her students in their morning ritual, the daily class pledge. A chorus bellowed out "I pledge allegiance to the A+ class. I will do my best at all times. I am here to learn and be smart. I will make myself, my family, and my teacher proud. I will always be respectful, responsible, and ready to learn for my sake and for the sake of those around me." And with that, students got to work. They headed to reading centers, where they worked independently on comprehension. When Sara wanted the entire class's attention, she interrupted their work with call and response. "A+ attitude," Sara called. Students stopped their work momentarily to respond, "Work hard, get smart!"

Sara lives and breathes the Teach For America standard of high expectations. She accepts no excuses from her students. Before students head into a nine-day school vacation, half of Sara's students come to Saturday school to fill in the gaps of what they'll miss during time away from school. Students and parents alike are invested in learning. Each week Sara assigns her students a family project as a part of their homework, in which families work together on creative thought projects. She starts the year with a family project of mapping the route from school to home. Their grades come from Sara's ability to locate their houses relying solely on their maps. Over the weekend, Sara follows the maps, shows up at students' homes with cookies, and introduces herself to the child's family. She distributes homemade refrigerator magnets with her phone number to all her students to encourage open communication. She invites individual families to her house for dinner throughout the year. Routine trips to the grocery store turn into informal parent conferences, as she runs into students and their families in the aisles or in checkout lines. The level of family involvement is impressive. Parents sew costumes for class plays. They show up to monthly Family Fun Nights that Sara runs at the local public library. In between bites of donated pizzas, students and their families play math games or they watch local high schoolers conduct science experiments.

Her commitment doesn't end with her individual students, but continues with the entire community. Sara is gifted in looking at problems and envisioning creative, thoughtful solutions. In serving on the

Board of Directors at a town domestic violence center, Sara writes a grant to fund art therapy. She creates a school chess club. When she notices the high levels of conflict and how her school lacks a resource to help students deal with conflict, she founds her school's community service club, the CARE team (Community Action and Responsibility Education). The ten student members that make up the CARE team train to be school leaders and to treat the world in responsible ways. They keep journals of their random acts of kindness. They carol during the holidays to collect canned goods for food banks. She takes her third grade class to a local retirement center, where students sing and partner with residents to make picture frames.

Sara's success is evident in her integral community involvement, as well as the academic achievement that is measurable in her students. In 2002, the average school-wide score on the IOWA Test of Basic Skills was in the 30th percentile in language arts. Sara's students averaged in the 72nd percentile. For math computation, the school-wide scores averaged in the 33rd percentile. Sara's students scored at the 81st percentile. After only two years in the classroom, Sara won the 2002 Wal-Mart Teacher of the Year award for the state of Louisiana. To nominate her, students submitted forms they collected from the customer service desk of their local Wal-Mart. Along with the recognition, Sara received $5,000 for her school.

Sara exemplifies how Teach For America's young, inexperienced teachers overcome adversity. In the following reflections, corps members evaluate their transitions to successful teachers, as well as their defining moments in the classroom. Their paths to success are not revolutionary. Rather, their success comes from vigilantly holding students to high expectations and investing students and families in classroom efforts. Corps members apply determination, perseverance, and hard work to overcome obstacles. Their stories show the limitless possibilities that corps members have achieved—that it really is possible for individuals in their first and second years of teaching (with only five weeks of pre-service training) to propel their students forward in dramatic ways.

high expectations

As a first-year teacher, Liz Marcell (1999, Rio Grande Valley) was assigned to teach a pre-school program for children with disabilities. Her students ranged in age from three to six, and had a wide range of exceptionalities, including dwarfism, delayed speech, spinal muscular atrophy, and attention deficit hyperactivity disorder. Of her thirteen students, two were classified as mentally retarded, two were diagnosed with cerebral palsy, and two had Down's syndrome. Other students were non-verbal, were born addicted to cocaine, or were the victims of abuse. Liz explained, "I had no training about special needs students. I knew nothing of their needs, their challenges, effective strategies, and the best ways to serve them." To complicate matters, Liz had no curriculum to guide her teaching:

> When I arrived, there was no specific curriculum. While my students were obviously well-cared-for, there was no sense that anyone held high expectations for them, or had much faith in their academic and social potential. My students spent most of their time doing activities that didn't push them in any way, or lead them to a point where time in the general education classroom could be a reality. The school community, and from what I sense, their former teachers, did not expect that my students could follow a relatively rigorous academic curriculum modeled after what was happening in the general education pre–K and kindergarten classrooms.

Despite these huge challenges, Liz's success was tangible. Out of thirteen children, six exited the special education program and moved into mainstream classrooms. How did she accomplish this?

First, true to the Teach For America mission, Liz held her students to high expectations and standards. Though her students were labeled as special education students, she constantly held them up to the standard of mainstream students.

My work was to get the word out that these kids could succeed. My kids were capable of doing normal things. They didn't need pitying. Pitying cripples children. When there are no demands on children, it limits their capabilities, hinders their growth and independence.

For Liz, teaching with high expectations meant creating a structured routine to teach students their colors, numbers, shapes, and letters. She planned out thematic units week by week, connecting art, science, and language arts in every activity. Believing that "kids succeed with routine," she reinforced ideas through repetition.

I wanted more structure. I wanted my classroom to be more similar to a mainstream classroom. I wanted to push my students in a way they hadn't been pushed before, rather than just babysit them.

Second, Liz became proactive.

I took the responsibility to educate myself about the specifics of my kids' challenges. The burden was on me to make success happen for my kids. I set about educating myself about my students and their disabilities. I worked with my administration to keep open lines of communication about what was going on in my classroom and what support I needed. I did research, talked with veteran teachers, spoke with parents, and special education experts.

Liz pointed out that mainstreaming students was no measure of success unless those students could keep up with their classroom peers.

The kids who moved out of special education completed their first year of regular education successfully. There was Crystal, who had poor motor skills as a result of cerebral palsy. She just blossomed in regular education. During my second year, Crystal came into my classroom and showed me her report card. Her report card was all Es—E for excellent. She had mastered every skill.

Liz Marcell has remained an active leader in the Teach For America community, serving as a Corps Member Advisor at the 2001 and 2002 institutes. Liz learned Spanish to be able to better communicate with her students' parents. She was voted "Teacher of the Year" in her school. As one of her student's parents said, "She really is an angel sent from heaven."

> *Success, as a teacher, is a breakthrough moment, when you know you've reached a child.*
> —Bill Norbert (1990, New Orleans)

Incoming corps members are advised that the first crucial step toward successful teaching is to create an ambitious goal for their students to accomplish. In the early years of Teach For America, goals were often nebulous and lofty. David Ables (1997, Bay Area) came to the classroom aspiring to "feel effective, like I could handle whatever was thrown at me." Sammy Politziner (1999, New York) admitted that his goal of "expanding opportunity" for his second graders was "amorphous, vague, and totally unhelpful in measurable strides." With accountability and measurability as buzz words in education, recent corps members create goals that produce clear outcomes in student achievement—goals like that of Dakota Prosch (2000, Chicago), who aimed for 100% of her sixth grade students to pass the Iowa Test of Basic Skills, and Nakia Whitney (1996, New Jersey), who aimed for 100% of her first graders to be able to read by the end of the year.

> *As a first-year teacher, it's hard to know what your expectations should be. It's better to have them too high than to not have them high enough.*
> —Kate Driscoll (1998, Washington, D.C.)

In the face of adversity, corps members learn to not lessen their expectations. Melea Bollman (1998, Rio Grande Valley) kept her expectations high because she believed in their power. "I really think they can do it, and I won't stop until they achieve these high goals." One of her proudest moments as a teacher came when she held a Creative Writing Open Microphone Night for her students in grades 3–5 with emotional and learning disabilities.

> The objective involved high expectations on many levels—both for my students and for their parents. I had been told that my students' parents wouldn't be involved, but I wanted them to share in the experience of seeing the results of their child's hard work. My kids told me that they couldn't write, but all of my twelve students stood up and read their work. Some wrote paragraphs and some wrote entire five-paragraph essays. All but two of the parents showed up.

> *The problem in Compton was a lack of high expectations for the teaching profession, which resulted in a lack of high expectations for the students. Everyone made excuses for why students in Compton would not be able to succeed. I tried to focus more on the possibilities for my students and giving them the opportunity to be challenged and motivated. I had high expectations for myself. I have never devoted as much time and energy into anything as I did with my teaching.*
>
> —Jason Unger (1992, Los Angeles), Winner of
> the 1998 Disney Teacher of the Year Award

Alan Giuliani (1994, Mississippi Delta) wrote the following essay about resisting the urge to lower expectations. The results of his classroom practices verified the positive power of high standards.

> A couple of weeks ago, I stayed after school with a student named Teresa. Algebra has not come easily to Teresa, but she has worked tirelessly. She cares a great deal about her performance. After big tests, Teresa typically calls me to see if I have graded her test. Perpetually behind, I have usually not graded it by the time she calls, but I always

promise to put her paper at the top of the pile. When I grade her paper, I call her with the news, whether it is good or bad.

Teresa's enthusiasm has played no small part in her improvements this year, but on that day a few weeks ago, Teresa's forward motion seemed stalled. She was about to take my pass/fail equations test for the fifth time. I demand that my Algebra II students take pass/fail tests for certain topics such as equations, integers, and fractions until they master them because knowing 50 or 60 percent of these topics just won't cut it. I view all my students as extraordinary, so they must know this material with world-class accuracy.

Teresa had taken four versions of the equations test already and had been close to passing all four—painfully close. I praised several of her excellent solutions on the exam—I really had been impressed—and then we inspected the errors together to see how she could improve on the next take. Teresa then took Form E of the test, spending a full forty minutes solving the equations and double-checking her solutions. As she turned in her test, Teresa was confident that she had passed.

She stood by me while I graded it, both of us nervous and excited. With three strokes of the pen, our hopes were dashed. It was clear that Teresa needed to retake the test yet again. I told her that she was a phenomenal, exceptional student for taking the test so many times, and I assured her that I had no doubt that she would pass the test soon, since the errors were so small. I launched into what was supposed to be an uplifting analogy about an Olympic track runner, but then Teresa couldn't hold her disappointment any longer. Teresa, the sweetest of girls, burst into tears.

I felt horrible. For the first time ever, I seriously considered saying, "Close enough! You passed!" Instead, I told her again that I knew she would pass. She nodded through her tears, and then we both called it a day. That evening I bought Teresa a card that stated Duke Ellington's mottos for success. "Rule 1: Never quit! Rule 2: Never forget Rule 1!" Then I wrote inside the card how much I admired her determination in the face of adversity.

The next day, Teresa proved unflappable and resilient. She came in, took her test, and passed it with 100% accuracy, much to our delight, and I'm sure, relief. Tears and pain fade. Cries of joy and pumped fists replaced the disappointment of past failures. Students like Teresa proved that great self-esteem comes not in watered-down standards but in the confidence that accompanies success.

My greatest success was in the classroom culture I created. My students learned not to say, "I can't do it," but rather, "I can't do it yet." I instilled the value and importance of hard work and discipline. Students respond when we give them respect and motivation.

— Michael Siegel (1999, Bay Area)

relentless pursuit

Yet other corps members measure their success by their abilities to open doors for students that previously were shut. In 1998, it was almost unheard of for students in the Rio Grande Valley to study higher-level science like physics. At Easton High School, only six to ten students took physics each year. Sarah Bezek (1998, Rio Grande Valley) and Anne Sung (2000, Rio Grande Valley) collaborated to change the situation. Anne began by explaining, to her school's guidance counselor, the necessity for offering high school physics. "We have students with interests in medicine and engineering and technical skills like mechanics. If students want to pursue any science career, physics is a valuable background," explained Anne Sung, a third-year teacher in her original placement.

They learn to apply math to science and use higher order thinking skills. Physics allows students to look at the world around them—how things move, light, sound, color—and find joy and excitement in explaining the aspects of the world through science. Moreover, colleges expect high school students to study physics, so to make the children of the Valley competitive, we must offer them physics.

The school administration agreed and funneled students into newly created physics classes. The numbers of enrolled students grew from forty in the first year to one hundred in 1999. In 2001, the numbers increased to 150 and now stand at two hundred students in both physics and AP physics. Anne expected students to be scientifically literate and to develop a scientific background that will allow them to read and comprehend books, articles, and discussions about science today. Anne's most tangible goal was for students to score 60% or higher on the Fourth Concept Inventory, a nationwide test that measures knowledge in the physics content area. Her goal was ambitious; in a typical college class, students score 20% to 40% on the same test.

> *As a teacher in Southern Louisiana, my greatest success was in exposing my kids to a whole new world that existed outside of the perimeters of their tiny rural town. It wasn't the norm for kids to move on past the bayou, but I made them think about it. I was always telling them, "Why not go to the University of Pennsylvania?" or "Why not Bucknell?" I encouraged them to ask themselves, "If you could go anywhere in the world, where would you go?" Then I made them strive for that goal. Gradually they got the sense that there was a whole world outside their tiny agricultural community.*
> —Leigh Anne Fraley (1992, Southern Louisiana)

Corps members apply relentless pursuit to solve obstacles through creative solutions. Melinda Manning (1994, Mississippi Delta) had no books to teach her fifth and sixth graders. Because there was no on-staff librarian, students were prohibited from checking out books from the school library. She overcame this obstacle by asking outsiders for help and was surprised by the generous donations she received. Undergraduate students at her alma mater led a book drive. Her family members and friends sent donations. The results were staggering.

> I remember when a box of books arrived at our classroom. It was like Christmas morning. My kids couldn't believe that they got a book of

their own to keep. For the first time in some of their lives, students were given their own books to take home.

For Christina Kelley (1994, North Carolina), success was bittersweet. When her students in the lowest track of high school English displayed spectacular growth on an end-of-course composition test, they were accused of cheating. Their academic success was doubted; to the school district administration, it seemed more plausible that underachieving students cheat than make actual academic strides.

Christina arrived at a Halifax County high school on the brink of a state take-over. Midway through the semester, Christina's tenth grade World Literature students would take an end-of-course test that involved writing a coherent and cohesive essay about world literature and using their literary analysis skills. In a class overflowing with up to forty-five students, Christina's students ranked in the 0–21 percentile on previous standardized tests and were rejects from the veteran English teachers' class rosters. Resources were scarce:

> My classroom had been raided before I arrived, leaving little more than a worn-out teacher's desk and not nearly enough textbooks or student desks. The pitiful books and desks remaining were sorely defaced, either by ink or chewing gum or both. Not to mention the cracked walls, cockroaches, and grimy floor.

Determination carried Christina to "achieve our goals despite others' obviously low expectations of us." She instituted a Saturday study session during which students could catch up or get extra help. She relied on nontraditional teaching and discipline methods to reach kids who hadn't been reached by traditional teaching methods.

> In general, school had never engaged these students. I wanted to change how my students perceived school and learning, to share my belief that education is a tool to be used by students for their own betterment. In the meantime, though, I would settle for adequate end-of-course test preparation.

With only six weeks to prepare for the test, Christina taught refresher lessons on basic writing skills and literary terms. She explained, "We read a great deal over the course of the semester, but we needed to get right to the meat of the course in the first two weeks." However, Christina faced dilemmas; "How does one quickly bring unwilling or resistant students up to speed, get them motivated to take and pass an end-of-course test halfway through the course, and engage them at the same time? Even if the students proved willing, would there be appropriate texts available to us?"

Christina linked her success to establishing relationships with school staff, veteran teachers, and community members. Her school librarian was a saving grace. The librarian secured forty-five copies of *The Diary of Anne Frank* and Elie Wiesel's *Night*. "I don't know how she worked such miracles in a school where the photocopy budget and cleaning supplies ran out in the first weeks of every semester, but we would have the necessary resources."

The following excerpt, written by Christina Kelley, reflects the accomplishments of her students and her resulting pride:

> The day of the end-of-course test arrived and my students headed to the library where it would be proctored. Under the watchful eye of the librarian and an assistant principal, my students wrote the essays I knew they were capable of. And more important they knew they'd done their best. We took a well-deserved break the next day. I never expected my students to be so persistent in their desire to know their essay test results. They ruminated, hypothesized, predicted, and agonized over how they did.
>
> With near delirium, I ran from the office to my classroom to deliver the amazing news: All students but two passed the test, a complete reversal of the previous year. And the two who didn't pass had just missed the mark and could still be very proud of their efforts. Students I never thought I'd see crack a smile ran around the class yelling, "I passed!" It was one of the happiest days of my life, too; I was so proud of my students. So it came as quite a shock to be accused by the central

office of cheating. According to one of the superintendents, there was just no way that these students could write essays with citations and page numbers, essays of such clarity and focus.

Now it was my turn to practice my own preaching; was I going to be depressed and apathetic or gather up the energy to make my students' fragile world a better place? The first people I spoke to were the librarian and the assistant principal who had proctored the test. They knew my students hadn't cheated. They had seen these usually jaded teens stand in a circle with clasped hands and heads bowed before the test; how could they forget? We were vindicated, but after the semester's end, somewhat tarnishing the brass ring we'd strived so hard to reach.

investing students and their parents

My students' parents expected me to be excellent. They would accept nothing less. They gave me their total and complete trust.
— Bill Murphy (2000, New Orleans)

Teach For America corps members realize that it takes more than ambitious goals to be successful. It takes investing students through meaningful lessons that inform, inspire, and engage. Maureen Kay (1999, Washington, D.C.) was determined to bring a civil rights unit to life for her second and third grade students at Baxton Elementary School in Washington, D.C. So she taught the ideas of social justice and activism not just during February's Black Awareness Month, but carried these ideals through the end of the year. Using Martin Luther King's "I Have A Dream" speech as a springboard, students drafted, revised, and rewrote their own speeches, focusing on how to bring about change and improvement in their communities and for their futures. The culminating step came when Maureen led her students in their own March on Washington, which brought the symbolism of civil rights into their worlds. Each student stood on the steps of the

Lincoln Memorial to deliver their own speech, just as Martin Luther King, Jr., had done so many years before them.

> *One morning, I was telling my students about an upcoming field trip to the New Orleans Zoo. I told them that they needed to get to school as early as possible because we were going to leave first thing in the morning. To emphasize my point, I started listing off all the aspects of the day that we would miss—daily test review, math mania, etc. The students started to look dismayed, and I asked Kearnisha what was wrong. She said, "Ms. Cotner, we're going to miss all our learning time!" I assured her that the field trip would be educational and that she didn't need to worry. Kearnisha thought about it for a little longer and added, "Well, can we at least bring flashcards on the bus?"*
> —Sara Cotner (2000, Southern Louisiana)

To the naive teacher, disengaged parents may appear an enormous obstacle to student success. But corps members often find the opposite: that through diligent efforts to invest parents through constant communication, weekly newsletters, positive and negative phone calls home, and home visits, parents are the teacher's greatest ally. Tom Shepley (1992, Baltimore) aspired to break down the separation between home and school. In his first quarter of teaching, he visited 80% of his students at home.

> I would walk kids home after school. I would wait at the front step and tell my student to ask his parent to come to the front door. Sometimes there was this awkward tension, but most home visits ended on a warm note. Moreover the people in the neighborhood would see me. Gradually people began waving to me. I didn't feel so afraid in a community that was so different than my own. I felt less like an outsider and more like a part of the solution.

Many corps members notice that community involvement facilitates community acceptance. Seth Morris (2001, Los Angeles) stepped out of his Compton classroom to visit ten families in the first months of teaching. Seth strived to develop an understanding and appreciation for students on an individual level, as well as their personal experiences and interests.

> I would call ahead and schedule meetings with parents, to send the message that their time was valuable. I wouldn't bring paperwork. Rather, I sit down with my student in their home environment and ask them about their life outside of school. What does he do after school? Who does he play with? What does he like to play? I worked with my parents so that they would realize learning was a joint effort between students, teachers, and parents. If any part in that equation fails, then the chances for success are lessened.

Seth made students' parents integral contributors in their child's education, teaching them how to fill out forms for library cards, inviting them on field trips, and leading after-school sessions to teach parents how to effectively read with their students, even for parents with limited English skills.

> I taught my parents how to ask their students reading comprehension questions. I taught them to have their child explain what they had just read. I told my parents how important it is to maintain their native language, how English isn't the only tool to success, how increasingly important it is for children to become bilingual. I hoped to empower my parents through sharing their culture and identity.

Seth's efforts to build community relationships resulted in invitations to baptisms, church, and parties.

My biggest success was that I became a part of my community. I felt I belonged there. I like to think that I was a leader in the school and that I helped my school move in the right direction.

—Jason Levy (1993, Houston)

Matthew Schmitt (1999, New Orleans) viewed the connection with his students and their families as his biggest success: "I truly believe that I was able to get into the fabric of the community, though it required so much faith, trust, and sensitivity on the community's part as well as on my part." In a speech delivered to his fellow New Orleans corps members, Matthew debunked the common myth that says parents are the scapegoats for poor student performance in classrooms.

> The most powerful statement that I encounter, probably on a daily basis, is, "These parents don't care enough about their children." I actually believe that this thought process is the larger problem, not the parents. It is not fair, and I find it to be a dead end in the road of getting students to succeed. If the bridge between school and home is burned, then what chance does a child have for any continuity in their education? Therefore, I refuse to believe that the parents don't care. Whenever I call my students' homes, I have found definite love and care in almost every single one. "Mr. Schmitt, she can't put her Harry Potter book down! She's reading!" And, "My son asked me to ask you what books I should buy him for Christmas." One parent actually broke it down for me, "I'm sorry if I was rude when I came into school, but I always hated school myself. I'm worried my daughter is just like me." This haunts me, because I wonder exactly how long this system has been failing its students. I know that the parents of my students care and love them very much. There are many factors that go into *how* they love their kids, how they might often be away from home so they can ensure food and clothes, how they might not be able to come hear their son honoring them at the Black History Month Awareness Assembly because of inflexible employers. But I don't find it productive to point fingers and place blame. Change does need to happen, a

change that draws strength from the good things that are already happening. There is much energy in those of us who are "doing the best we can." I believe there is enough to begin the necessary momentum.

Matthew explained that "In my first year of teaching, I started calling parents all the time. I would call ten a day until I called them all, and then I'd just start the cycle over again." Through an open dialogue with parents, Matthew noticed immediate results: "I became a voice in the community. Suddenly I had all this authority."

After two years in New Orleans, Matthew Schmitt left full-time teaching to pursue a career in music: "I needed a step back from teaching so that I could learn how to be more balanced before returning again." He worked for the Los Angeles Teach For America regional office and he currently teaches with Educating Young Minds, a non-profit learning center which offers home-study day classes, after-school tutorials, weekend remedial classes, and S.A.T. preparation assistance for inner-city Los Angeles children, grades K–12. He also hires new teachers through the Los Angeles Teaching Fellows program and helps with a non-profit after-school music program that transitions students from juvenile detention back into school. He displayed his enormous admiration for his students and the larger New Orleans community, stating, "Everyday I think about moving back. New Orleans is a place that never leaves you." Matthew estimates that he remains in touch with eighty students and their families.

determination

I was on a personal mission to help the really tough kids, the kids who needed me the most. It took absolute and complete devotion. It took getting administrators and parents involved. It took not giving up on those kids.

—Clare Pinchin (1999, Bay Area)

Lamott was my most challenging second grader. Just thinking of him makes me laugh. He was very bright, but also very angry and disruptive. His father wasn't in the picture, and you could sense some of his anger stemmed from that. Lamott was very charismatic, but he just refused to follow directions. I remember one day chasing him around the room. He was literally hiding under desks. But I kept working on him. I would tell him, "What you're doing is not right, but I'm not going to give up on you." I stuck with him. He began to come to me after school and we worked on writing and storytelling. We worked to turn his skills in a positive direction. It took a while, but he definitely started to come around. I took him to after-school activities and a mentoring program. By the end of the year, he was not perfect by any means, but he was with me. He was on my side. His mother sent me a card to thank me for all my time and effort. The next year, his teacher came up to me. She told me that he was doing exceptionally well. She told me he was an ideal student. Lamott was the student who needed my time and effort the most.

—Tim Gamory (1995, New York)

Erica Larsen (2001, Los Angeles) was challenged by her kindergarten student Joseph, who came to her classroom refusing to speak. In the following speech, "Joseph Talks," delivered at the 2002 Teach For America Los Angeles Gala, Erica's patience and her steadfast confidence in her student were the components for success.

My first day as a kindergarten teacher, and my student list was missing from the front office. Having never taught before, I could not have known how essential it was. Without it, I had no way to limit the 37 four- and five-year-olds who suddenly became "mine." Of those 37 little bodies, there was one in particular that caught my attention early— Joseph Reyes. I noticed him quickly, he was the only one of the 37 who wasn't constantly chatting away. I soon found out from talking to other teachers that this was not Joseph's first time in kindergarten. He already had one year under his belt with a veteran teacher at my school. During the previous year, he never once spoke to his teacher. He had been observed talking with his peers, but his little voice had never been heard by a faculty member. I knew what I had to do. I had to help him find his voice, and show him how to use it, in and out of the classroom.

After three weeks, my class was reduced to a manageable 30 students. Soon after, I contacted the parents of each of my students. I spoke with Joseph's mom extensively, both on the phone and when she would pick him up after school. She was concerned not only for Joseph, but for his twin brother Gary as well; Gary never spoke to his kindergarten teacher either, but somehow he had made it to the first grade. Every day after school his mom would ask me, "*Le habla Joseph?*" and everyday I had to say, "*Todavía no. Pregúntame mañana.*" (Not yet. Ask me tomorrow.) When I suggested coming to her house to see Joseph at home with his family, his mother seemed unsure. Joseph was most tight-lipped when both his mother and I were present. A home visit would be our last resort.

By the end of October the morning meeting routine of my classroom had been established. After journal-writing, a few students shared their journals with the class while sitting in the "Author's Chair," a privilege coveted by all, except for Joseph. We then sang songs that would help students learn the days of the week—an adapted version of "Happy Days" was a classroom favorite. Using Popsicle sticks to call on each of the students equally and randomly, I drew Joseph's name out of my cup. "What day is it today, Joseph?" No response. "Is it Wednesday?" No response. "Thursday?" Once again, no response.

"Teacher, Teacher, Joseph talks!" said Gabriela, a fellow student after recess one day in November. "I know he does, Gabriela. Let's help him talk to me in the classroom." That afternoon, with Joseph in earshot I told his mother that anytime I heard him speak he would be rewarded by a sticker. I soon found out that Joseph was not one to be so easily persuaded by rewards or enticements. For all of my efforts, time seemed to be my only ally. By Christmas, Joseph was answering yes or no questions by shaking or nodding his head. There was hope for 2002.

Each day we had to spend an hour and a half on Direct Instruction, a scripted reading and language program. This was usually the most trying time for me and my students. For Joseph it was particularly grueling because it was completely oral. Joseph was undoubtedly intelligent and creative. By January, he was showing great strides in his journal-writing. He drew detailed pictures of his family and his friends, and was even beginning to spell pre-phonetically, making attempts to sound out letters and words in his head. But when it came to Direct Instruction, he completely shut himself off to me and often disrupted other students as he sat restlessly in his chair. That is why I was shocked when, one day, he tentatively began to respond along with the other students. I had to restrain myself from jumping up and hugging him right then and there. In fact, I did the opposite and pretended I didn't hear him. I wanted him to be comfortable with his voice first. When my impatience got the better of me, I asked him individually to identify his colors aloud. He quietly told me each and every color, including gray and baby blue.

By the end of the month, Joseph was speaking to me in front of the rest of the class. When I asked how many syllables there were in his name, his little voice replied "three." I was glowing. The other students seemed happy for him and for me. After all, Joseph had been speaking to them since the beginning of the year. It was the teachers he wouldn't speak to. In March, Joseph orally identified all of his letters and their sounds. We were outside in front of the school and his mom was watching, listening closely. She and I were so delighted and very relieved. We hugged each other and sandwiched Joseph in between us.

In April, Joseph volunteered to sit in the Author's Chair and tell the students about the story he had written in his journal. He told a story of when he went to the zoo with his grandparents and saw a huge snake eat a rat. Joseph truly did find his voice and his smile. When I see him at school this year, he grins from ear to ear. When I ask him how he is doing, "Fine," he giggles, and scurries off to his first grade classroom.

It takes more hours, it takes building relationships with students and their families. It takes being visible in the eyes of the community— going to student birthday parties, and church, and football games, and shopping in the local grocery store. It takes a commitment to being at school early in the morning or late into the evening.

—Ray Owens (1990, Los Angeles)

First-year teachers succeed because of their persistence, resourcefulness, and determination. Persistence comes from working long hours and never giving up. In her first four years of teaching, Michelle Koyama (1997, Rio Grande Valley) arrived at school at 6:30 am every morning and rarely left before 6 pm.

> I have many memories of the custodians kicking me out so they could set the school alarm. I was often at school on Saturdays and I almost always brought paperwork home with me so I would not take the time away from my students.

Resourcefulness is doing whatever it takes to make achievement happen for students. Jay Hartling (2002, Baltimore) rifled through school closets at eleven o'clock at night to ensure that books landed on desks for every student. Determined corps members never stop from reflecting on their teaching practices and seeking out professional development opportunities. Carissa Nauman (2000, North Carolina) applied constant learning to her teaching practice every day.

> I reflected and analyzed and learned. That was how progress happened. I had very little support from mentors and veteran teachers, so really it was all about the slow process of learning what works and what doesn't work and applying those tricks of the trade.

Clare Pinchin (1999, Bay Area) became aggressive in seeking out what she needed. After enrolling in a credential program, she continued to attend weekend workshops on classroom management and math conferences.

> *John was a seventh grader in my classroom. I knew he was capable but he had slipped through the cracks. I spent my heart and soul with him. John was always there after school. He worked and worked, and he got his grade up to an A. He became interested in learning, whereas before he was falling asleep. At the end of the year, I asked him to sign my yearbook. He wrote, "Thanks for believing in me when no one else did."*
>
> —**Carissa Nauman (2000, North Carolina)**

Just as there are stories of corps members who achieve classroom success, there are an equal number of corps members who realize exactly how hard the Teach For America experience is, who understand how arduous it is to change the status quo of public schools, and who remember the day-to-day battles. In their candid opinions about the difficulty of teaching, some corps members confess to not being successful. For Amy Christie (2001, New York), her challenges with classroom management made her first year a struggle to survive: "There would be days when I felt like I hadn't taught anything. It felt like this fruitless effort, even if I had planned for hours. There were days when lessons crashed in my face." She grappled with her own frustration and intolerance. "Sometimes I felt like I had lost myself. As I was screaming at eight-year-olds, I would think, 'Where is the person who was once so idealistic?'" Derek Redwine (1995, Houston) regarded his first year of teaching as "a complete waste. I don't know what I did for those kids. It was a huge wash." Scott Joftus (1990, New York) remembered being "squashed" in his first year:

> I got run over by that first year. I didn't know the tricks of the trade. My classroom felt like absolute chaos. I felt like I failed my fifth graders because I couldn't effectively teach them how to read. It was hard to go home every day with that feeling.

Sherry Wagner's (1998, Washington, D.C.) two-year struggle made her question her perception of Teach For America:

> I wouldn't say my years teaching were a success. I think Teach For America looked at people like me as a failure, because we were not bringing our students up 1.5 grade levels, like they had told us to. Teach For America doesn't want corps members to think that the realities and the circumstances matter, but they do. It does matter that I taught nine students who were in foster care. No matter how well you are trained, the circumstances of poverty, of learning disabilities, and of low abilities do matter.

Similar circumstances made Karen Buck (1996, Southern Louisiana) doubt her ability as an effective teacher. In a high school with caved-in ceilings, rickety desks, and pervasive gang problems, she struggled to teach a disruptive group of eleventh graders. "I realized that I wasn't the teacher I thought I'd be. I was more formulaic and taught from a book and worksheets just to keep control of my students." These realities led Karen to wonder whether she was accomplishing what she had originally set out to do. Eventually Karen began to think, "It seemed like I couldn't do another year." At the end of her first year, she resigned and opted to not return for the second year of her Teach For America commitment. Though she was careful to not blame Teach For America for what she believes to be her "own failure," she sensed that "to some extent, Teach For America makes it seem that all it takes to be successful is effort." From her experience, Karen concluded, "It takes more than effort. It takes a special type of person."

And though Teach For America readily highlights the success stories of their corps members, there are voices of skepticism who question corps members' ability to achieve classroom success. These voices come particularly from within graduate schools of education, who assert that uncertified teachers, including TFA corps members, have lesser impact on their students than do certified new teachers. In September 2002, Professor David Berliner of Arizona State University released a study that found that "the students of uncertified teachers had 20% less growth in their achievement on standardized tests than students with a traditionally certified teacher." The study matched pairs of teachers from similar placements, similar schools, and similar districts. Uncertified teachers—including Teach For America corps members—were each matched with a newly hired teacher, but one who had been through a traditional teacher preparation program. Berliner explained:

> Teach For America is a failure in producing the kinds of achievement its public relations would have us believe. As a group, Teach For America produces less student growth than that of traditional teacher training. I'm not defending that certification is the only means to getting qualified people into the classroom, but if we pose the question, Is Teach For America failing? then, yes, they are.

chapter seven

outside the classroom

On a Saturday morning at 8:00, first-year teacher Susan Asiyanbi (2001, New Jersey) is in an unlikely place. Rather than lounging in bed on a weekend morning, she drives through the neighborhoods of Jersey City, New Jersey, and arrives at school, where a group of fourth grade students greet her. Susan spends the next thirty minutes eating breakfast with her students and chatting about movies, basketball teams, and wrestling. Students hand Susan tapes and CDs of their favorite songs, and she plays them while students sing and dance. She watches and claps along, encouraging her students to "shake it out," to get their energy pumping and minds awake and ready. At nine o'clock, the music is turned off and Susan shifts into teacher mode, splitting the group of twenty into two smaller groups. They head into two different classrooms and the day begins at the ESPA Academy.

As a rookie teacher, Susan came to a New Jersey elementary school in which only 8% of students passed the Elementary School Professional Assessment (ESPA) standardized test. Right away, Susan set goals for her students and her classroom. She envisioned a safe and nurturing environment in which students felt emotionally comfortable to talk to their teacher, to support each other in learning, and to address their classmates with respect and understanding in weekly class council meetings. To invest students in their own learning, she gave students monthly agendas to map out their learning. Students predicted their own learning and projected the skills they wanted to gain. Susan introduced each lesson with a clear objective so that students would understand how it related to larger learning agendas. Each month ended with a benchmark test that enabled students to gauge whether they had mastered concepts and ideas. To prepare her students for the ESPA, Susan made test preparation creative and stress-free. She relied on games to encourage critical thinking skills and to teach solutions to multi-step math problems.

Back at ESPA Academy, students reach for their coats and head outside to begin their math and science explorations. Susan tells her students to gather seven leaves, and they do so. She poses a question, "You have seven leaves. Four of them blow away and you collect six more. How many leaves do you have?" Hands go up as students are eager to display their understanding.

Through this creative approach, Susan translates success to student achievement. At the end of her first year, 32% of fourth graders pass the ESPA. Moreover, Susan's involvement outside the classroom helps her to work more effectively inside the classroom. Extracurricular involvement gives her the chance to know her students better. Her parent connections strengthen as a result of ESPA Academy. Students, who may otherwise dread coming to school throughout the week, scamper to get out of bed on Saturday mornings. Parents, who may have been skeptical at first, understand Susan's investment in their students' education. Susan has exceeded the call of duty in proving that she "will do whatever it takes to better educate these students."

For many Teach For America corps members, the commitment to students does not end with the 3:15 bell. Many find the school hours are too confining when it comes to student achievement. They maximize out-of-school hours to provide students with meaningful academic and extracurricular opportunities. In a survey conducted by Teach For America at the conclusion of the 2001–2002 school year, corps members reported the following:

- More than half of corps members led existing extracurricular activities in their schools, while more than a third started new extracurricular activities.
- Nearly 50% of all Teach For America corps members participated on a school improvement committee and almost 50% of those assumed leadership positions. Additionally, of this group, more than one in three corps members have started school improvement committees where there were none.
- Over half of all corps members secured grants or other resources to compensate for financial limitations of the schools in which they teach.

These statistics translate into corps members like Kate Driscoll (1998, Washington, D.C.) who led Rainbows, a support group for children who had undergone a significant loss—for example, their parents' divorce or the incarceration of a family member. Nakia Whitney (1996, New Jersey) served as the vice president for her school's Parent-Teacher Association, and Mark Pett (1994, Mississippi Delta) worked after school with his sixth graders to publish a newspaper that circulated to the entire student body. Corps members arrive early to provide extra tutorial sessions. They give up their only free periods during the school day to invite students to join them for lunch. Scot Fishman (1997, Washington, D.C.) spent his evenings coaching his elementary school's boys basketball team on to winning the district championship. Allison Serafin's (2001, Houston) weekends consisted of Girls and Boys Nights Out, when she went to the local movie theater to hang out with her students. Some corps members don't even rest during their sacred summer vacation. Melinda Manning (1994, Mississippi Delta) formed a summer writing program at her middle school, where students of all ages spent three weeks practicing and improving their writing skills.

academic enrichment

I'll do whatever it takes. School doesn't end at 2:30. My students come to me an hour before school for extra math help. They stay an hour after for reading intervention. Some kids get seven extra hours of schooling a week. That's the only way to do it.

—Dakota Prosch (2000, Chicago)

By December of her first year, Nakia Whitney (1996, New Jersey) witnessed her kindergartner Michael read. Not only did Nakia realize the limitless potential of her students, but she also reassessed how much time and effort were needed on their behalf to make her entire class readers. The STAR Club—Sharing the Art of Reading—was the result of Nakia's thought and preparation. "I must admit that I started the club for selfish reasons. I didn't want my own inadequacies as a rookie teacher to hold my students behind." Nakia paired up with a fellow Teach For America corps member, who taught at a neighboring high school. After school, the high schoolers came into Nakia's classroom to read with her kindergartners. The club included not only Nakia's students, but also their siblings. On a typical afternoon, thirty-five elementary schoolers read with their high school mentors.

One Friday night, we had a reading sleepover. Ten corps members and I took kids from three grades and camped out in the school. We stayed up all night telling each other scary stories and having a reading marathon.

—Jason Levy (1993, Houston)

In her high school English classroom, Wendy Eberhart (2000, North Carolina) was determined to sell her kids on reading. Creating a love for literature went hand-in-hand with a love for writing and language. Feeding off her students' enthusiasm, Wendy worked with her freshmen to create a literary magazine. To cover the expenses for publication and circulation, students raised $1,500. "Not only did it allow my students to practice their creative writing skills, but it gave me the opportunity to implement team building, group discussions, and interpersonal skills." Moreover, students chose and revised selections, edited submissions, and printed the magazine with minimal adult guidance. The project culminated in a coffeehouse performance, which pulled together students from many arenas of the school. "My students had so much ownership over the project that there was enormous pride."

In an effort to return to the basics, Sammy Politziner's (1999, New York) Bronx elementary school provided no curricula, standards, resources, or time during the day for science and social studies classes. Sammy's solution was Project YES—Youth Exploring Society. In between his first and second years of teaching, Sammy led a summer camp focused around community exploration and investigation. He and his Teach For America colleague Emily Stauffer (1999, New Jersey) created a curriculum about citizenship—why people come to America to live, as well as how citizens in New York's different neighborhoods live. The objectives were multifold: to encourage students to think critically about social studies issues, broaden the horizons of students who had never explored their own city, and provide a safe, engaging learning environment in the summer months.

Sammy began by writing a proposal and securing $4,000 in grants to jumpstart Project YES. He chose four students on the merits of their intellectual curiosity. For three days a week, Sammy met these students at a local subway stop at eight in the morning. En route to their destination, students read articles from *The New York Times*. They scanned subway cars and advertisements to look for examples of persuasive writing. They spent their mornings doing experiential hands-on learning. Students visited Ellis Island and the Statue of Liberty. Lunchtime brought journal writing and playing in New York's many public parks. To integrate vocabulary lessons, Sammy took students to the midtown New York Public Library, where they leafed through dictionaries. He constantly asked them to use math skills in figuring out distances between city blocks. At no cost to students, Project YES provided lunch, souvenirs, and kid-friendly treats.

By his second year of teaching, the camp expanded to two sessions a summer, serving a total of nine students. Camp extended to four days, rather than three, and Sammy hired other teachers to help lead campers. To apply, campers wrote about their interests, their learning objectives, and the places in New York they wanted to visit.

Also in the second summer, Sammy revamped the curriculum to address social studies standards and to incorporate the idea of equality of opportunity. Project YES worked with community-based organizations to explore the opportunities in New York's neighborhoods. To explore the experiences of Jewish immigrants, they visited the Lower East Side Tenement Museum. Their explorations took them to Harlem, Chinatown, the Upper West Side, and Washington Heights. To figure out what life was like for neighborhood residents, students interviewed people, collected items from the neighborhood, and took pictures with cameras bought with grant money.

Over the course of the summer, students understood the disparity of life in New York's neighborhoods, that not all residents had the same opportunities. Students then turned to how they, as third graders, could work to solve the problem. They brainstormed several solutions, primarily communicating about the depth of the issues. To vocalize the problems, students spoke to reporters, politicians, and the mayor. They wrote letters to the governor and president. A social activism component came next, in which students made sleeping bags for the homeless, read to preschoolers in city shelters, and worked at a local food bank. To culminate their studies, students gave presentations to funders and parents. The last day of summer camp took students to a Yankees game, in a celebration of their learning.

Through Project YES, Sammy "took control and become a successful teacher. It was one of the first times all the participants met the goals I had set. It improved my teaching." Project YES is now a nonprofit organization, which has expanded to serve students in New York and Louisiana. After two years, Sammy left his original placement because "I had no interest in working at a school that was failing its students, that wasn't meeting the needs of its population, and that wasn't doing good things for kids." Project YES piqued Sammy's interest outside of school time. "Outside of the school structure, my success was, in part, tied to my autonomy." His interest in public school reform through the venue of after-school time led Sammy to Harvard's Graduate School of Education. "I am interested in combining my deep value for experiential education with an equal passion for educational equity. I'd eventually like to be a school leader who creates a standards-based, experiential education school serving students from under-resourced communities." He maintains two personal visions: to create a Saturday mentoring program focusing on students in first through fifth grade and their progression through high school and a charter school focused on cross-country travel with middle schoolers. In the 2003–2004 school year, Sammy returned to teaching and hopes to take on an administrative position in the near future.

In her second year of teaching, Nicole Curinga Iorio (1992, Baltimore) focused on improving the social climate at her southwest Baltimore elementary school. Once she noted that fighting was a daily ritual for students, she approached her principal with an idea: the creation of a school-wide student intervention program. Thanks to a principal whom Nicole regarded as a "commanding, caring, genuine, innovative leader," Nicole was given the go-ahead to use already-secured grant money to fund the project. Nicole applied the funds to a three-year program which combined conflict resolution and peer mediation. Nicole oversaw the project—planning budgets, arranging materials, scheduling speakers, and coordinating faculty training.

Nicole envisioned alleviating aggression to improve the climate. Fourth and fifth graders were trained as peer mediators and were on-duty in areas where fighting frequently broke out, like the hallways and the cafeteria. School-wide assemblies gave students new ideas on how to avoid aggression through problem-solving strategies, conflict resolution, and peer mediation. Students learned to use "I care" messages and to rely on words, rather than fists. Teachers were encouraged to rethink the ways in which they interacted with students, and how they could incorporate effective strategies to build classroom communities. Over the course of one year, school violence declined. Nicole explained, "The school began to take on a quieter, more secure feel. Students and teachers alike learned how to interact in a positive, respectful manner."

Nicole spent three years teaching in Baltimore and worked at two Teach For America Summer Institutes. She traveled to Guatemala to teach at an international school, before settling in New York. After working as a literacy coordinator at a non-profit organization, Nicole turned to combining her passions of writing and education. She now works at *TIME Magazine For Kids* and is completing her Masters in Psychological Foundations of Reading from New York University. She credits Teach For America with giving her "a tremendous background in learning how to do any job" as well as giving her a direction to pursue her skills and interests. In her current work, she writes material that reaches 3.5 million students.

First-year teacher Maia Heyck-Merlin (1999, South Louisiana) came to the classroom with an immediate challenge. For the first year ever, Louisiana relied on a high-stakes test, the Louisiana Education Assessment Program (LEAP 21), to determine whether students would be promoted to the next grade level. The LEAP, administered to students in fourth, eighth, tenth, eleventh, and twelfth grades, tests students' basic and higher-level thinking skills. Immediately Maia recognized that her fourth graders would be retained unless they scored proficient marks on the test. This fueled her sense of urgency to help kids catch up to grade level and communicate the importance of the test to her students' parents. She "hit the ground running" by investing students and contacting parents by phone and home visits. With the help of other fourth grade teachers, Maia created a Saturday school program that focused on test prep skills. Students were given diagnostics to group them by level and spent Saturday morning reviewing skills, critically thinking through questions, and familiarizing themselves with the test. Attendance rates were high as parents began to understand the seriousness of the test and supported Maia's efforts. Breakfast and lunch were provided and in the spring, a recreation component was added so that kids stayed all day long. The results were profound. By the end of the year, 85–90% of Maia's students passed the Language Arts portion of the test.

While in the classroom, Maia also worked to create a school-wide positive reinforcement system and to implement writing workshops with other teachers. After completing her commitment, Maia stayed in Southern Louisiana to teach at a charter school and then became the Executive Director with Teach For America's regional office. Much of her efforts now focus on creating the infrastructure to allow the corps to expand in the region and establish relationships with new school districts. She doubts that she will "ever be able to pull away from public education" and sees herself returning to the classroom as a teacher or as an administrator. Maia currently works as the Institute Director for Teach For America's summer institute in Houston.

First-year teacher William Stubbs (2002, North Carolina) believed "across the board, standards have been lowered for students. When that happens, students slip through the cracks and are not prepared for college and life." To reinforce high expectations, a sign above William's door read, "Enter into this classroom an inquisitive individual." The sign on the reverse side of the door read, "Leave this classroom an informed individual." His teaching philosophy is, "If I can't get to them in the classroom, I'll meet students in the community to get them up to par." Only three months into his first year of teaching, he identified students who needed his attention the most, students in need of role models and character development. Determined to spend time with those students outside the classroom, William attended town parades, band practices, and brought students to church. He and a fellow Teach For America corps member established weekly tutorial sessions at a Hardee's restaurant in town. William approached restaurant managers to secure their permission for using the restaurant as a meeting place, to which the managers willingly agreed. Thereafter, the district superintendent heard about the additional tutorials and supported the two corps members monetarily, compensating the teachers and purchasing food for the students from the restaurant. William explained, "In essence, both the community establishments and the school system have partnered to propel the success of students."

school clubs

On an average day at Walker School in Northwest D.C., the ringing of the lunch bell brings students into Brian La Macchia's (1998, Washington, D.C.) science classroom rather than the cafeteria. "Mr. La Macchia," they ask, "Can I get a chessboard?" Brian patiently puts his sandwich down and rifles through cardboard boxes to hand out bags of chess pieces and the corresponding boards. Brian is responsible for the school-wide chess craze that has swept these middle schoolers.

In his first year of teaching, Brian invited a teacher from the U.S. Chess Center into his classroom to begin basic chess instruction. Immediately kids were hooked; "Kids that were good at chess were the ones who weren't good in the traditional school setting. It was their way to prove to themselves that they were smart and capable of beating their classmates who were getting better grades." Feeding off the frenzy, Brian began keeping students inside once a week for formal instruction during recess. Gradually he put together a small team to take them to D.C.'s elementary team chess league. In the weekend tournaments, Brian and his students were an "anomaly. The rest of the tournament was rich kids and their parents." The competition, however, upped the ante for students who would "lose and return to school to raise their games."

The excitement was contagious. "For some kids this was the first time they were really excited about something that was happening at school." Not only did chess teach students problem solving, prediction, and recognizing patterns, but Brian incorporated the formality of the game and its manners into instruction. "These kids were used to seeing competition of showboaters. In basketball today, the kids see an athlete gloat over his victory. They translated victories into flaunting.

Here, I stress manners. They shake their opponents' hands and sincerely congratulate each other." In two out of Brian's four years, Walker School won second place in the city-wide D.C. Schools Chess Competitions. One year the school secured a first place victory. More significant than any title is the interest that chess has sparked among his students. "I have had parents come up to me and report that their child asked for a chessboard for Christmas."

> *I created a basketball league, which was very important for the academic and behavioral performance of my sixth graders. In order to participate, students have to keep a B average. They must have ten positive phone calls home a month. The kids get so excited. They couldn't believe that my partner teacher and I got so involved. They hardly expected me to slap on my Nikes and join them on the court.*
>
> —Justin Arnold (2001, Los Angeles)

The time came when Payton Carter (1999, Bay Area) "took off his tie, loosened up a bit, and began to discuss shared interests with his kids." He stopped in the hallways to check out students' dancing, which was a part of the school's hip-hop culture. The results were the formation of a high school breakdancing club, founded in 1999. "Students knew about my interest in dancing, and they approached me to see if I would be the faculty leader of their club. They did most of the work themselves—electing officers, writing a constitution that was ratified by the student council." Payton's students started friendly competitions with clubs from neighboring schools. The club gained so much recognition that *The Source* magazine wrote an article about them in the spring of 2000. "Kids were being recognized and given this sense of authenticity. I remember one kid took a picture of himself from the magazine and ran down the hallways holding it over his head." The article sparked even more media attention when ESPN asked students to perform for the 2000 X–Games Opening Ceremonies. To prepare for the games, thirty students practiced three times a week with Payton's guidance as well as assistance from UC Berkeley students who had been breakdancing for years. On the day of the performance they met and performed on the same stage as celebrities, rock stars, and professional wrestlers. Payton will never forget one of his students telling him during the taping, "Mr. Carter, this is the best day of my life."

At the end of the day in San Benito, Texas, children and teachers filter out of classrooms, through the doors, and head home. However, for rookie teacher Liz Marcell (1999, Rio Grande Valley) the day isn't over yet. The after-school hours bring students to her classroom for a Multicultural Art Club, which Liz co-founded with Melea Bollman (1998, Rio Grande Valley). When art classes were limited due to budget cuts and a district-wide push to return to the basics of reading, writing, and math, Liz witnessed a void. What emerged was an art club to provide a venue for hands-on art instruction and activities, with a unique focus on the world outside the Rio Grande Valley. "My students had limited knowledge about the world outside of the Valley, and art was a way to expose them to new worlds." Students meshed the arts with global studies and created African tribal masks and Italian fresco paintings. They wrote Japanese haiku and decorated their poetry with Japanese-influenced watercolors. They made Mexican clay pottery. They beautified their school and the surrounding community by painting murals and making mosaic tiles to cover the school picnic tables.

outside school hours

It's mind-boggling to see how rookie teacher Alissa Naymark (2002, Detroit) got it all done. Life as a first-year teacher was a juggling act of taking classes toward certification, attending school basketball games on Saturday mornings, and constantly reflecting on how to reach a goal of having 75% of her students pass the Michigan State Standardized test. In between grading papers, spending nearly an hour each night phoning students' parents, setting up science labs, and trying to unpack her new apartment, Alissa somehow managed to serve as a team captain for the nationwide Cybermission Science Competition.

This was no ordinary science fair. Created by the Chief of Staff of the United States Army to increase student achievement in science, math, and technology, it went beyond making volcanoes explode from vinegar and baking soda. In this Web-based competition, seventh and eighth grade students combined their expertise in math, science, and technology to solve problems in their communities. For example, students inquired about the health and safety implications of using basketball shoes, which are largely designed for wood court surfaces, on asphalt.

On Wednesday afternoons, students reported to Alissa's classroom to work on their science projects. Teams were comprised of three students, who pooled their knowledge to formulate questions, research solutions, and submit the application online. Students chose a topic from one of four categories: arts and entertainment, sports and recreation, health and safety, or the environment. Alissa served as their sounding board and their compass in pointing them toward resources. For a February deadline, teams had to submit their research documents, and I-videos all online. If they won at the national level, each student would receive an $8,000 e-savings bond.

Coming to McAllen, Texas, Caitlin Wittig (1997, Rio Grande Valley) became painfully aware of the high levels of need in the impoverished area, yet the lack of proactive solutions already in place. Fueled by her own interest in political action, Caitlin inspired her alternative high school students to seek out action and begin their own student-centered community projects, where they took immediate action through their own planning and implementation. In teaching self-empowerment, Caitlin assisted her students in organizing peace rallies, mural paintings, and non-violent marches in honor of Martin Luther King, Jr., and Cesar Chavez.

> These projects gave the kids a real sense that they could change something. They could act upon their world. These were students who had

always been forgotten. They were students who had always been labeled as not good enough. They were students who had babies of their own, who had messed up with the law, who had previously dropped out of school. This program allowed them to become examples of good public servants.

Through Caitlin's leadership and the awarding of grant money, the program merged into Do Something, a nationwide community service program teaching leadership through curriculum and service learning. Students were taught to look at their communities and take action to make them better. With the enormous success of the project, Caitlin shared the program with ten neighboring schools and trained fellow teachers and administrators.

After school and on the weekends, all I was doing was hanging out in the community. Many weekends, I would fill my truck up with cans of paint and meet kids out in the city. We'd cover up graffiti on neighborhood walls, fences, and bridges.

—Jason Levy (1993, Houston)

outside school walls

Though Mark McClinchie (1996, Houston) left his Houston middle school after five years, his legacy lives on through *Clase Sin Paredes*— Classroom Without Walls. Struck by the apathy that pervaded his school and the lack of programs to serve students, Mark set out to establish a disciplined, structured classroom that would promote academic skill building. He turned his conviction that learning must continue beyond classroom walls into an enhancement program that brought students to the forefront of exploring educational outlets beyond their hometowns.

The program began as a before- and after-school enrichment project, in which students spent one hour before school strengthening skills in novel reading, literature, and current events. Two hours after school were spent on community service projects, service learning, and the occasional field trip. Thirty middle school students read to kindergarten students and nursing home residents. The end of the year culminated in a trip to Boston, which Mark regards as "the highlight of my teaching career. The kids truly earned that trip. They had worked so hard." It was only with the reassurance that Teach For America corps members would continue CSP that Mark could comfortably decide to return to his hometown of Pittsburgh to continue his teaching career.

Sure enough, fellow corps members, including Lisa Leadbitter (1997, Houston), Martin Dust (1996, Houston), and Stephanie Newton (1995, Houston) joined Mark's effort in 1998. The four teachers shared equal responsibility in sending fifteen students and their chaperones on a five-night trip to Washington, D.C. Students took advantage of D.C.'s learning opportunities, including memorials and museums. In 1999 with the success of the Washington, D.C., trip and a subsequent trip to New York, Mark founded CSP in the fall of 1999. He ran the program for two years, until he passed it off to two 1998 corps members, James Sheridan (1998, Houston) and Phil Wright (1998, Houston). In recent years, Houston students have traveled to California and Hawaii. Clase Sin Paredes is still running in its Houston middle school, now carried on by two 1998 Teach For America alums.

How can a high school French and Spanish teacher instill a passion for learning and a love for language in the minds of her Southern Louisiana students? For Amy Jennings (1997, Southern Louisiana) the answer was obvious: a twelve-day all-expenses paid field trip to Barcelona, London, and Paris.

As a first-year teacher in the small rural town of Crowley, Louisiana, Amy realized her students faced academic, geographic, and cultural isolation. She brought the romance languages alive in the classroom with French and Spanish films and music, but was not satisfied with just that. Her goal was for her students to communicate and maneuver in a new language and environment. Though her academic expectations were high, she believed a love for language and valuable life experience would come only from a trip to Europe. She knew her goal was possible; corps members before her had done similar projects, giving her a sense that this was feasible even in a small town.

In her second year, Amy created the Romance Language Club, which was open to all high school students. Initially 170 students signed up, though the final numbers whittled down to 40. Students' parents were expected to attend meetings and assist in fundraising efforts. Students raised money and community support through car washes, bake sales, door-to-door efforts, and handwritten letters. Moreover, Amy partnered with a local bank and opened up individual bank accounts for each student. Students who did not meet their fundraising goals kept the earnings they had raised, as a way to encourage students to save for college. Eighteen students raised $37,000 to pay their way for a spring break trip to Europe. The end result was a direct link between hard work and big rewards.

Though Amy regarded the trip as "an amazing experience," it brought a sobering reality about her own naive assumptions.

> I wanted to take my students to Europe and have them independently maneuver there without me. When we arrived in Paris after having relied on public transportation in London and Barcelona, I, as well as the other chaperones, handed my students maps of the city and told them to choose whatever they wanted to do, wherever they wanted to go, and to get us there. I was shocked. My students got angry, some of them cried. They didn't take advantage of the opportunity, but instead they freaked out. It made me realize that being measured as a teacher meant what my students could do without me, not what they were capable of only through me.

Amy Jennings left the classroom to pursue educational leadership, with the realization that advocacy for her students meant taking on an administrative position. In 1999, she became the Program Director for Teach For America in the San Francisco Bay Area, overseeing support of first- and second-year corps members. She held the position for four years, but left to earn her Principal's Certificate at Harvard's Graduate School of Education. Ultimately, she plans to return to the Bay Area and has set her sights on becoming the principal at a school that has changed principals every year for the past four years.

Autumn De Vos (1997, Baltimore) brought Spanish to life for her Baltimore sixth, seventh, and eighth grade students. As a first-year teacher, Autumn aimed to bring students on a week-long trip to Mexico to study the culture and improve their language skills. Autumn was mentored by TFA alum Tammie Nielsen (1996, Baltimore), who brought six students on a week-long trip to Mexico in June 1997 with "Project Mexico."

Tammie and Autumn began the 1997–1998 school year with a grand vision: to expand Project Mexico not only in the number of participants, but to make it a two-school effort with both elementary and middle school students. Project Mexico began as a traditional after-school club, though lessons soon turned to studying Mexican culture and history. Students, with their sights set on a week-long trip to Mexico, completed an application complete with teacher recommendations and letters of intent. Weekly meetings focused on fund-raising efforts toward a goal of $30,000. Tammie and Autumn secured grant money from Baltimore businesses while students held bake sales, organized school dances, and sold candy to their classmates, to their families, and to the surrounding community.

But Project Mexico was more than just an after-school club. It was a seven-month approach in which students developed language skills, broadened their global awareness, and set personal and academic goals. With community support, the students reached their fund-raising goals and boarded a plane to take them from Baltimore to Mexico City. For the next week, eighteen students were immersed in Mexican culture and language. They toured authentic markets where they mingled and bargained with natives, they climbed the Teotihuacán pyramids, and they swam in the Caribbean Sea off the beaches of Cancún. Autumn witnessed the benefits of the trip:

It was a great way for students to learn. They learned more than I could have taught them in a traditional classroom setting. There were so many levels of learning. They saw a different land and culture. They experienced different foods. They met and talked with people who seemed different on the surface, and then they discovered that they weren't really so different. It opened their eyes to the possibilities of new worlds, and they compared that world and made connections with their own lives.

community involvement

In his second year of teaching, Jeffrey Max (1999, New Orleans) was disappointed to find a lack of school community among teachers and students' families. Jeff's solution was to plan a community event, which doubled as a fund-raiser for resources the school desperately needed. To integrate elements of the region's culture, Jeff planned a Crawfish Boil.

He began his work in December by spearheading monthly meetings among teachers. His fellow teachers quickly caught on to the idea and their energy spread to the student body. As the date grew nearer, students sold tickets to their families and the surrounding community. There were school-wide contests to see which class could sell the most tickets. Students made and posted signs around the school and the community. They set up games for children to play at the event. Each class made a mural to display their schoolwork. Jeff worried how selling tickets among residents of low-income neighborhoods would be perceived, but he realized through parent involvement and their support how much parents cared about the welfare of the school. Jeff secured additional funding from outside sources, as well as donations from the regional Teach For America Board of Directors. Jeff regarded the Crawfish Boil as a huge success. Over twelve hundred pounds of crawfish were enjoyed by teachers, students, and families. The net profits reached $2,500, which was used to buy a much needed copier machine and library materials. Jeff Max left New Orleans after his two-year commitment in hopes of pursuing a long-term solution to the problems he witnessed in the classroom. He is currently working toward a Masters in Public Affairs and Community Development from Columbia University.

Jennifer Jefts (1997, Rio Grande Valley) believed that service learning, hands-on learning to provide service to others, was the best teaching method for her students. She secured $10,000 in grant money to create a school-based food pantry in Edcouch, Texas, managed and staffed by seventh and eighth grade students. Initially students served families for one hour a week, with meals being served every other week. Thirty students worked to serve over two hundred students a week. More grants were secured to fund the food bank's expansion. Students were involved in every step of the process: interviewing clients, assisting families in filling out applications, ordering and packing food, and running fund-raising events to pay for additional food. All academic areas were integrated in each step. Students relied on math skills to measure and weigh food and they depended on their social skills and writing skills when filling in client applications. Each family was tracked in a computer database to gauge the frequency of their visits.

Though Jen left teaching, the food bank survived. She remained in the region continuing to work in the field of service learning. She now works as the Program Director at the Americorps Youth Harvest, a program that works with one hundred high school seniors from six districts in the Rio Grande Valley. These high school seniors become AmeriCorps volunteers and log over nine hundred hours of community service to earn a $5,000 living stipend and $2,300 in educational awards. Participants tutor and mentor within schools, and volunteer time in community sites like libraries, public housing sites, and Boys and Girls Clubs. In addition to their service hours, students attend monthly meetings to prepare them for leaving high school. AmeriCorps Youth Harvest was awarded the Governor's Volunteer Award in 2001 and now serves as a model for which other schools base their service learning projects.

In both traditional and innovative ways, corps members take leadership roles, commit long hours to student achievement, and bring their students to learning opportunities outside of classroom walls. These ambitious corps members prove that the power of a teacher extends far beyond reading comprehension and arithmetic lessons, that teachers and students can measure success in ways other than the scores on standardized tests.

chapter eight

two plus years

The Teach For America group in my home state did a wonderful job, and a lot of these kids wind up staying and teaching, even though they can make two and three times as much money doing something else.
    —Former President Bill Clinton at a 1999 education summit

I want to always be a part of the fight, the struggle, the movement for equality. Education is the way to do that.
    —Matthew Schmitt (1999, New Orleans)

Though Teach For America demands a two-year commitment, a self-reported 60% of corps members remain in the field of education—40% in the classroom and 20% in educational leadership and policy. Of the alumni still teaching, nearly half are still in their original placement school or community. Seventy-five percent of teaching alumni work in public, non-charter schools, 15% teach in charter schools, and the remaining 10% work in private schools. In a 2003 survey, 81 alumni reported that they have founded a school. Here alumni reflect on the variety of reasons that lead to their decisions to continue working as educational leaders in many forms: teaching in original placements and regions, working in newly formed schools, taking on school leadership positions, and working in educational policy to bring about systemic reform.

alums in their original placements

At the end of each year, I would think "I didn't do that well enough." Ultimately I decided that I needed to stay until I felt that I got it right.
—Amy Wilson (1992, Baltimore) on her decision to stay in her original placement for five years

I stayed after two years because there were a lot of things that I hadn't yet achieved with my students.
—Melinda Manning (1994, Mississippi Delta)

Much of Michelle Koyama's (1997, Rio Grande Valley) decision to stay in teaching was influenced by her relationship with one student.

After my two years I decided to stay for a third year primarily for Edgar. Edgar was a third grader, who I taught for two years. We had made significant gains academically. I wanted him to have a solid fourth grade year in order to transition smoothly to fifth grade. Edgar had a lower-than-average cognitive ability. I really pushed him in reading, writing, and math. I was terrified that he would not get another special education teacher that would have the same expectations that his parents and I set forth for him. Then, after three years, I just became so invested and I stayed in my original placement for five years.

Michelle Koyama believes her experience planted the seeds for working with special education students. She is currently pursuing a masters in special education, while working on teacher training and supervising beginning teachers. She has maintained her connection to Teach For America by working at four summer institutes.

Payton Carter (1999, Bay Area) stayed not because of a commitment to one student, but rather a commitment to his entire first-year freshman class. In his application to Teach For America, Payton checked a box indicating he would be willing to work as a special education teacher, with the thought that "It can't hurt. It will show that I have an open mind." Really Payton assumed he would teach high school history, his field of study in college. Instead Payton was assigned as a resource specialist teacher—a placement in which special education students are pulled out of mainstream classrooms to receive specialized instruction—with a caseload of twenty-eight students with mild to moderate learning disabilities.

Payton confessed to his own naivete:

> At first, I was hesitant to teach special education. I didn't really even know what it meant to have a learning disability. The institute opened my eyes to the range of disabilities. I still remember being moved to tears when I was trying to teach Donovan, a Houston fourth grader, the letter names. We went over and over them again and again, and all Donovan could do was rub his eyes. I tried to empathize. I tried to imagine what the world looked like through Donovan's eyes. It was the first time I realized the different ways in which students process information.

What resulted was Payton "falling in love with the kids, with the school, and with the job." Payton felt an immediate bond with his students who were "so interesting, so outgoing, and often had the best personalities." He worked with students like Ricardo Garcia, a ninth grader who was so nervous about school that he simply didn't come. Payton first convinced Ricardo to come to school, then assessed him to find out that Ricardo, at the age of fifteen, was on an early first grade reading level. Payton worked closely with Ricardo until he picked up over three grade levels in reading ability and his confidence skyrocketed. Recently, Payton shared in Ricardo's victory of passing his written driver's license test.

Payton's decision to stay past his commitment stemmed from a vested interest in his first group of students, who in June 2003 will graduate from high school. Fifteen of his original caseload of twenty-eight students will earn their diplomas. In his fourth year of teaching, Payton Carter was promoted to the Special Education Department Head at his Oakland high school. Along with other corps members, he helped to prompt Teach For America to reassess how applicants are placed in special education positions, resulting in a process that requires a more open dialogue and a more conscientious decision on behalf of the applicant. He is simultaneously working toward a master's degree from University of San Francisco, in Mild Moderate Disabilities. His goal is to be "a teacher that hopefully these kids will remember as someone who worked sincerely for them."

> *In those first two years, I grew and learned so much. I wanted to go even further. I was an okay teacher, but by no means was I that TFA superstar. In my heart, I knew that this was right, so I kept doing it. It wasn't really even a question.*
> —**Carissa Nauman (2000, North Carolina) on her decision to teach past her two-year commitment**

Not only do corps members feel an obligation to their individual schools, but like Alan Giuliani (1994, Mississippi Delta), to original placement regions as well. Alan's connection to his region and his community ties were possible because of his rural placement and his intricate involvement in a small town. He began his TFA experience in Helena, Arkansas, where he taught high school math for five years. He left to pursue his degree in administration from Harvard's Graduate School of Education, and returned to the Delta to continue teaching, this time in Indianola, Mississippi:

I never thought I would pursue a degree in school administration. But in those beginning years of teaching, I found myself always writing down notes of all of the things that I would change if I were in charge. There were simple structural changes I would make, and larger instructional revisions. But it got me thinking that even I could make a difference as an administrator.

Upon graduating from Harvard, he returned to the Delta to teach, not be an administrator:

I could have gone anywhere, but I chose the Delta again because of the tapestry of relationships that I gained being in a small town. As a fifth year teacher, I was somewhat of a celebrity. I liked walking into Wal-Mart and being recognized and feeling loved. But I returned to the classroom because I wanted to teach for several more years before I tried to lead a school.

Alan Giuliani is one of the estimated 16% of the 1994 Mississippi Delta corps who remain teaching in the area.

Steph Crement (1999, Bay Area) came to Teach For America thinking that "education would be the great leveler. It was the answer to social change." Instead she had a "depressing realization that the education system, the way it is set up in so many public schools, wasn't the avenue to change. It was perpetuating the cycle of poverty." Her decision to remain in East Palo Alto schools was her determination to "keep working at this. My second year felt successful. I stayed to investigate more. I stay today to find the answers to some pressing questions: How can students come out of our public schools with the same skills as the wealthy students in Palo Alto schools? What's going on here? How can it be fixed?"

There are so many amazing kids—that's what keeps me teaching. Even kids who may give you trouble do beautiful things.
     —Katherine Onorato (1999, Oakland) on her decision to stay in her original placement for four years

Andy Shin (1999, Bay Area) attributed his decision to stay past his two-year commitment to the great progress he witnessed. In his first two years of teaching at an Oakland middle school, there was a tremendous amount of staff turnover, including principals who left mid-year only to be replaced by substitute administrators. In his second year of teaching, the school "hit rock bottom. There were so many fights on campus that there was just a feeling of violence." Andy pointed to that year as the turning point:

> People took note of how bad things had gotten. The community stepped up to help us out. Church groups came in to help. Oakland community organizations came to teach conflict resolution. People from within the school district offices came to monitor the hallways in passing periods. It was like the community came to help us, asking "What can we do?"

As a result, the school set to work on its underperforming school intervention plan. In the late spring of his second year, Andy and a group of his fellow teachers visited a middle school in a neighboring district that had recently undergone drastic improvements:

> Here was a school that was just like us, in our student populations, with the same sense of chaos before. They had adapted a new curriculum, based on integrated thematic instruction and collaborative learning. It was remarkable. The school was beautiful. There was this warm school community. There were exciting and engaging lessons going on.

Andy resisted the temptation to join the small school movement that was making huge strides in Oakland public schools. "I certainly thought about leaving to work at a small school. But I saw these small schools that were working, and I began to care more and more about my school. I wanted my school to work." In his third year of teaching, Andy worked with a new administration and a core group of teachers hoping to integrate an innovative curriculum.

There is more consistency now. There is so much planning and looking toward the future. It's been a bumpy transition, but there is always a forward-looking focus. As a school, we are learning to look ahead to where we are going. There's a new sense of energy. It feels like we are on the cusp of a big breakthrough, big improvements. Sometimes I get frustrated with how slow the change feels, but I know this is a long-term process. Already there are improvements in the school climate. The fights are decreasing and instead are being replaced by this new sense of calm.

This gradual change and improvement has kept Andy at his original school site for four years. Andy concluded with the optimism that "in a few years, things here will be really great."

alums as lifelong teachers

Other alums reveal that their simple passion for teaching has been the decisive factor in their decisions to stay in the classroom. What began as a two-year commitment for Nick Foote (1993, Houston) has turned into nine years in the classroom. Placed in Houston, Nick spent three years teaching special education elementary students. Upon leaving, he taught in Madison, Wisconsin, and Phoenix, Arizona, where he worked with a team of other educators to open a charter school. He currently teaches first grade at a charter school in East Palo Alto, California. Nick's decision to continue in public education was based solely on his lifetime passion for educational reform.

I am inspired and moved so much by what I do. I believe in this so much. After all these years, I remain convinced that children need teachers who push them forward and beyond toward greater things. I continue in the classroom today because of my opportunity with Teach For America. They put the key in the door for me. I turned it and went in.

Nick's commitment to educational excellence exceeds classroom walls and even school doors. Nick is a powerful community member who helps his students and their families.

> I met with the vice presidents of banks to help my students' families set up bank accounts. I talked to landlords to get my students' families leases. I worked to find low-cost dental care for my students and their families. I did whatever I could do to help these families be competitive in the system of laws and rules and regulations.

Because of his tireless efforts, the Sun Prairie School Board of Sun Prairie, Wisconsin awarded Nick the Results Plus Award for going beyond the call of duty to serve students and their families. Satkaur Khalsa, the parent of one of Nick's former first grade students, offered praise for the "zillions of benefits" that came from Nick's teaching:

> Most teachers come into the classroom thinking "Here is the material I need to teach." Nick was a gift to us. He found out who each child was and how he could reach them. He reinforced cultural diversity and made my son proud of who he was. He saw my son's brilliance and found a way to tap into it while preserving his self-esteem in the face of what he couldn't do. Nick taught mind expanding and interesting things with a broader perspective. He always took a profound interest in my son and my family and their ambitions. He was an extraordinary teacher.

Many corps members use Teach For America as a springboard to careers in education outside their original placements. Take Murray Carlisle (1997, Mississippi Delta), for example. Two years in the Delta and a master's in teaching led Murray to teach at an alternative high school in the mountains of Transylvania County in North Carolina.

> Many students come to us because of behavior problems, which translate to academic problems. We provide them [with] a program with

small class sizes—ten students on average. They get constant supervision, as well as a closer personal relationship with their teachers. We have much more of an open dialogue with our students.

The school provides an on-site counselor, drop-out prevention programs, learning labs, and a service learning project implemented through mountain biking and trail maintenance. As a result of small class sizes and its comprehensive offerings, Murray's school has the top test scores of all alternative schools in the state of North Carolina.

Yet not all Teach For America alumni continue in teaching placements that mirror their original schools. Sometimes corps members discover that the challenges of poor urban and rural schools are simply too great, and they move on to more stable schools. Jeanetta Mack (1995, Los Angeles) came to Teach For America to "be able to try two years of teaching." Although she assumed she'd be well prepared for her placement, she quickly discovered that "Compton was not like I imagined. My students had really different life experiences than my own. I just didn't have any hands-on experience. I didn't know what to do when you have a student crying under a table, and she refuses to come out." Three to five of her students lived in a group home, which neighbored the school and "the idea of students in my class not having parents or guardians was foreign to me." What got Jeanetta through those two years was a combination of putting in long hours, consulting with other teachers, and teaching through trial-and-error.

Jeanetta completed her two-year commitment and returned to her hometown in search of a school with better training, with professional development opportunities, and with excellent teachers reaching high standards with their students.

As tough as it was, as much as I knew I wasn't meant to be an inner-city teacher, I knew that working with kids was incredibly rewarding. I saw that through hard work I could positively affect children. Kids are truly the future, and that's where I wanted to focus on social change.

In her eighth year of teaching, she currently works in a suburban school and feels that she is a more focused, better prepared educator because of Teach For America.

> Now I have a clear understanding of what the standards are. Now I have successful strategies to get my students to those standards. I teach my third graders to learn how to work with their peers, and to develop a love for reading, math, and writing. I want them to recognize that they have a lot of options in the world and to encourage them to try new things. I want them to become resourceful people who can go about finding things that interest them to be successful people in whatever way they choose.

Yet other alums continue on in education at a higher level. Art Schuhart (1990, New York) is a lifelong educator in a very different venue. He came to the 1990 charter corps after reading an article about Teach For America in *US News and World Report* and thinking, "'That's what I'm going to do.' I was so sure that I'd be with Teach For America that it seemed a foregone conclusion." Though he only completed one year of his commitment, Art left New York to earn a teaching certificate and continue teaching in Washington, D.C., independent of Teach For America. In seven years of teaching in a Washington, D.C., public high school, he served on the city-wide textbook selection committee, as the Chair of the English Department, and procured a $100,000 grant to create an on-campus writing center. Seven years, however, took its toll and as much as he loved teaching and his students, he left "sick at heart over interacting with school bureaucracy."

Art is working toward a doctorate degree from George Mason University in community college education and focusing his dissertation work on writing textbooks for secondary and college composition courses. Now as an assistant professor in composition and literature at Northern Virginia Community College, he points to Teach For America as the reason:

I ended up doing what I'm doing today. Teach For America gave a person like me, who didn't know what I was doing, the opportunity to discover that not only did I enjoy teaching, but that I didn't want to do anything else. It gave me an immediate support network that cushioned the first classroom experience. It gives corps members a reflective outlet and a side door to enter teaching to discover that they are good teachers.

alums as school leaders

I realized that the majority of the decisions that affected my students came from the administrative level. To protect my students from bad decisions, to see changes take place, to truly impact their lives, I felt I had to go higher. That leads to the path of educational leadership.
—Amy Jennings (1997, Southern Louisiana)

Excellent schools require excellent leaders, thus prompting many TFA alumni to pursue roles in school leadership and administration. After seven years of teaching, Jill Levine (1992, New Orleans) worked as an educational consultant and became an assistant principal. Now Jill is the principal of a newly created museum magnet school that serves 230 elementary school students in Chattanooga, Tennessee. Magnet schools are created by public schools as a way to create choice in public education. Though the school follows district mandates about hiring, testing, and accountability measures, it has autonomy regarding its curriculum and philosophy. Affiliated with six city museums, the school's curriculum uses museums in the place of textbooks. Every Tuesday, students embark on learning expeditions to museums. Student projects are recorded in an electronic portfolio.

Jill believes her work in educational leadership is a direct result from her Teach For America experience. Jill points out the common myth that children from high poverty backgrounds aren't capable of academic success and how her TFA experience negated that myth.

Teach For America made me want more for children. I saw children who were in dire need of the best possible education. Through TFA, I saw that students were overcoming in spite of the obstacles before them. I realized that children were excelling, once they were offered more possibilities. Kids need high quality opportunities wherever they are and if those opportunities exist, they will succeed.

Jason Levy (1993, Houston) is in a unique position. Not only is he a Teach For America alumni with eight years of classroom experience, he now serves as an assistant principal in New York's District Ten. In his South Bronx elementary school, he oversees seven first-year Teach For America corps members.

His decision to leave teaching for administration was difficult. "In my last year of teaching, I realized that I couldn't exert the amount of energy I wanted at the pace I wanted." Jason, however, wanted to remain connected to public education. "I had experience in public schools. I saw a system with many flaws but so much potential. I wanted to make a difference from within." Though he misses the hands-on approach and teaching on a day-to-day basis, he appreciates his ability to be involved in decision-making and influencing the larger picture of public education.

In his second year as an assistant principal, Jason was excited to learn that Teach For America would place corps members in his school. He offers corps members the perspective that "things take time" in becoming an effective teacher. He has also been impressed by the progress and work ethic he has witnessed:

Two months into the school year, I can see great things happening. The potential of corps members is palpable. They are already making inroads in teaching kids to be passionate about school and life. They are starting clubs, coaching sports teams, and taking students on college visits. They really want to make a difference, but they're also frustrated in that progress might not happen in two months or even two years. They're starting to realize that their commitment might be more of a beginning than an ending. Corps members really want to inspire their students for the short term and the long picture, not just for the test on Friday, but for the test they'll take in high school. I'm glad that corps members are at my school and they'll only get better.

Jason holds a master's in educational administration from Columbia University's Teachers College. He served as a Corps Member Advisor at two summer institutes, explaining that, "It's about giving back. As much as I got from other teachers, I gave back to incoming teachers." As an assistant principal, he hopes to hire additional corps members, to facilitate a strong relationship between his school and Teach For America, and to retain corps members in a supportive school environment. "If you guarantee a wonderful experience and training, a chance for individuals to grow and to lead, I will bet on them wanting to stay for more than their two-year commitment."

Hae Sin Kim (1993, Bay Area) has never rested from her struggle to bring about educational equity for the children of Oakland, California. After six years of teaching in and leading the special education department at her original placement school, she earned a master's in administrative planning and social policy and a principal certification from Harvard's Graduate School of Education. She returned to Oakland to become an assistant principal and a key player in the founding of ASCEND, a new small school which opened in 2001.

At the time of her return to the Bay Area, Oakland Unified School District was undergoing massive revisions. Frustrated parents and the Oakland Community Organization (OCO) initiated a grassroots movement to create new autonomous schools, or small schools. Oakland's small schools serve a population who typically attend overcrowded and underperforming schools. In a community known for its social activism, the Oakland small school movement grew out of political mobilization. Hae Sin explained:

A large group of parents were angry about the conditions of the schools. They were encouraged by Oakland community organizations to commit to change, to mobilize and organize for real reform. Additional support came from the Bay Area Coalition of Essential Schools (BAYCES), who was interested in district-wide reform. Parents and interested teachers went to target schools in New York and Chicago to develop a vision and spark people's energy around the possibilities. Too often dysfunctional districts are heavy with blame-finding, hopelessness, and a sense of defeat. Here all the pieces of the puzzle fit to regain a concept of possibility and hope. We had interested parents, BAYCES, OCO, the superintendent, the school board, and educators all on the same page and wanting to collaborate. It's the collaborative nature of the work that's powerful.

Hae Sin is now the principal of ASCEND, a small school which serves two hundred students from K–8 with a projected growth to 360 students. ASCEND's goal is to prepare kids to move forward, with the conviction that race, ethnicity, and socioeconomic class hold no bearing on a child's achievement level. With a bird taking flight as their symbol, ASCEND students are given the message that flight from home will enable them to launch, gain perspective, and see new places. "It's not about the flight home. It's about flight as in attaining height where height is equated to achievement. Educational achievement in our society opens doors, allows access to new opportunities." ASCEND adheres to true community in an effort to have kids see a seamless connection between home and school. Even discipline is seen through a new lens, in which students are given responsibility to take ownership over their own actions and the ramifications of their actions on the larger community. Fighting and cursing is replaced by students helping each other. The curriculum includes yoga, capoiera, and art classes. Students are allowed to roam the campus without the constraints of many traditional schools. In seventh grade, students begin to explore college—what it means, how college is related to power, and why college is a strong option. By the end of the year, they have seen ten college campuses, where they go on scavenger hunts to interview people about the admissions process, the academic experience, and diversity issues.

When it comes to judging her school's success, Hae Sin remains both optimistic and realistic:

> At ASCEND, we measure our success through the strong culture. Students are proud. Parents are happy. We rely on parent input and participation and our community is satisfied. But this is inadequate. It's easy to say—"Look, we have a clean school where everyone is happy." Because many of the students and families and even the teachers have existed in such dysfunctional settings, we have to use many more measures to self-assess—their test scores, their day-to-day work, parent involvement, teacher satisfaction, reflection, survey, and a zillion other sources of data. We use a system of checks to show that all data points toward progress.

Hae Sin concluded that in her ten years in Oakland, this is the first time she has been surrounded by an infusion of hope.

> Energy is starting in pockets, but it's growing. There is a district-wide movement to make schools more autonomous. People recognize the promise we are showing and opt to come to Oakland to be a part of that progress. And it's all thanks to community mobilization—that's what makes Oakland continue to move. When communities work for grassroots action, that's how change will happen.

alums as school founders

Other Teach For America alums have moved to the forefront of educational leadership by creating small schools and charter schools geared toward producing high student achievement in low-income neighborhoods. In particular, alums like Xanthe Jory (1996, New York) have been proactive in procuring charter schools as a means to increase choice for parents and students in public schools.

A native New Yorker, Xanthe Jory returned to the South Bronx upon earning her BA from Stanford University. For three years, she taught fourth grade while working toward a master's in elementary education from CUNY Lehman. Her classroom experiences in her third year of teaching lead her to her current position, founder and Executive Director of the Bronx Charter School for the Arts, opening to 160 students in September 2003.

Xanthe admitted that founding a charter school "wasn't in my long-term plans and it was actually more of an accident. But since then, it has become my dream to open a school." When she thinks back to her third year of teaching in the South Bronx, Xanthe recalls spending her lunchtime fantasizing with other teachers about how things would be different if they were in charge of schools.

> I was frustrated, I was planning to leave teaching. I was working as hard as I could as a teacher, and yet came across so many barriers that prevented me from having the impact I wanted to have.

At that time, New York passed a state law creating provisions for the establishment of charter schools, public schools that receive state funding on a per-pupil basis, but are independent of local school districts. Charter schools have autonomy in staffing decisions, budget control, and curriculum. To maintain this autonomy, charter schools enter into a performance-based contract with the state, based on student achievement outcomes.

> We have to set clear measurable guidelines about our outcomes, and our funding is based on our ability to meet those outcomes. Our kids will have to take state-mandated standardized testing. We have to follow certain state regulations, about issues like special education compliance, serving students for whom English is a second language, and admitting students through a lottery not based on academic ability, race, or income—though following these mandates is certainly not problematic. But when it comes to our school design, our methodology, and our philosophy—we have freedom.

Xanthe began with securing an initial grant of $5,000 and joining a team of other educators to develop their vision for a charter school. In the early stages of the planning period, Xanthe earned her M.Ed. in administration, school leadership, and school development from the Harvard University Graduate School of Education. She spent a year visiting schools and working through collaborative efforts to create a vision for a school, including its mission, philosophy, and structures. The result was a charter elementary school that integrated the arts into curriculum, located in the artistically vibrant community of the South Bronx.

In July 2000, the team submitted its proposal to the New York City Board of Education, as it was undergoing tumultuous transition and changes in leadership. After seven months, there was no action on the proposal. In February 2001, Xanthe and her team withdrew the proposal and resubmitted it to the Board of Regents, the statewide governing body for schools. The process of procuring a charter was taxing:

> It felt like the Board of Regents changed the rules in the middle of the game, and we were always dealing with the funding question. No charter schools—in New York—can exist solely on state-granted funding, but funders won't commit to you until you have your charter.

When the Board of Regents finally addressed the proposal, they returned with a plethora of technical, substantive, and compliance-related questions. After twelve months, ten rounds of amendments, and a resulting eight-hundred-page proposal, in March 2002 the charter passed. Simultaneously, funding from outside foundations came through.

The Bronx Charter School for the Arts subscribes to the mission that arts education is a catalyst for the academic and social success of all students. Housed in the Hunts Point neighborhood of southeast Bronx, the student body is representative of its surrounding community in race, ethnicity, and socioeconomic background (99% of students in neighboring schools qualify for free lunches). A random selection process ensures that all children are eligible. Parents submit applications and students are chosen by lottery. Already, Xanthe has seen "an enormous interest level." BCSA relies upon music, drama, dance, visual arts, and crafts as individual subjects but also as integral components in the subject areas of reading, writing, social studies, science, and math.

Xanthe is confident that her work with establishing a charter school was almost "all Teach For America inspired."

> Teach For America was a vehicle to get me into education. I'm not sure if it is the field I will be in for the rest of my life, but certainly for a long time. I feel positively about the organization. It played a formative role in my career development. I looked to Teach For America for its philosophy—high standards, a non-defeatist attitude, an endless sense of possibility, and the notion of urgency.

As she witnessed fellow Teach For America alumni in leadership roles in New York City public schools, Xanthe concluded, "Teach For America has created an energized group of young educators. Thanks to them, new things are happening."

JoAnn Gonzales (1997, Rio Grande Valley) had a vision of a charter school in which middle school students thought about college. Her ideas stemmed from an after-school program she had started in her second year of her commitment. In the program, students committed time before and after school to increase academic achievement. JoAnn teamed up with fellow TFA alum Tom Torkelson (1997, Rio Grande Valley) to make this vision a reality for the students of South Texas. The result was Idea Academy, a charter school created in January 2000. In the school's second year, they received the 21st Century Learning Grant. The grant enabled the school to keep students for extended hours, pay for additional tutors, and bring in local artists to work with students.

The Individuals Dedicated to Excellence and Achievement (IDEA) Academy is the only state charted public middle school in Texas' Rio

Grande Valley, offering students in grades 4–8 a dynamic college preparatory education. The school is working "at the grassroots level to transform a community ravaged by gangs, drugs, and violence." Since its founding, the school has served 180 students, the majority being Mexican-American and 90% qualifying for free lunches.

The crux of the school is community involvement, revealed even by the school's founding in which parents, students, and teachers rallied support for powerful alternative education options. School leaders "do not hesitate to put themselves in the community and let parents know we need their presence." The community relationship is very much a reciprocal one that is mutually beneficial. Evening English as a Second Language classes as well as babysitting services are offered to parents.

The school's philosophy is that college readiness will come as students attend school longer, work harder, and receive more hours of quality instruction. As a result, test scores on the Texas TAAS test have skyrocketed. In 2001, 98% of students passed the math test and 91% passed reading. Scores on the writing test rose in one year from a 58% passing rate to 90% passing. On alternate Saturdays, students work on service learning projects to empower themselves by transforming their communities. There is also a strong arts integration, including raising moneys to start a school symphony. Students work each year to earn a "golden ticket" which allows them to go on end-of-the-year extended field lessons, trips to Washington, D.C., camping trips, and trips to tour colleges and universities in Texas.

In its third year, over 50% of IDEA's staff are Teach For America veterans. JoAnn Gonzales credits Teach For America as her stepping stone into education, as well as showing her that "no matter where you are, learning is a continuous process for educators themselves." She believes Teach For America's powerful influence is its ability to "create a strong network of mentors and people who are working toward systemic reform:

> I feel very indebted to TFA. Without it, I wouldn't be in the Rio Grande Valley. Without it, this school wouldn't exist.

One of the most powerful creations of the Teach For America alumni network is KIPP, the Knowledge Is Power Program, founded in 1994 by two former TFAers Mike Feinberg and Dave Levin. Like Teach For America's mission of educational equality and adherence to high standards, KIPP is dedicated to providing educationally underserved students with the knowledge, skills, and character needed to succeed in top-quality high schools, colleges, and the competitive world beyond. Students are held to high expectations for academic achievement and conduct. KIPP students, teachers, and parents create a culture of achievement. Students have access to teacher phone numbers and a toll-free 800 number to ask homework questions. KIPP students complete two to three hours of homework nightly. KIPP schools rely on a longer school day, an extended academic year, and summer school. KIPP students spend 67% more time in classrooms than other students, with school days starting at 7:30 and running until 6 pm. KIPP focuses on results through test performances and measurable objectives. Only two years after their formation, KIPP New York and KIPP Houston were recognized nationally as notable schools. KIPP Houston was named a Texas Exemplary School in its first six years of operation, and its students consistently score among the highest rankings on the TAAS, the Texas state exam. KIPP New York has met similar success, being one of the highest performing middle schools in the Bronx. Ninety-nine percent of KIPP students attend college preparatory high schools.

Since its 1994 founding, KIPP has evolved into a national non-profit organization, teaming up with school districts and state education departments to incorporate KIPP into public education systems. In 2000, founders Feinberg and Levin created the Fisher School Leadership Program, a year-long training curriculum in which candidates receive business training at the Haas Business School at UC Berkeley, rotate through and observe in KIPP network schools, and return to their sites to begin the six-month start-up preparation.

Rich Barrett (1996, Houston) took his TFA training and re-created Teach For America's leadership model in KIPP schools across the country. After teaching for two years at his original placement, Rich moved on to KIPP Houston, lured by KIPP's warm, friendly atmosphere, its strong sense of structure, its balance of fun and discipline, and its administrative support. His experience at KIPP was so positive that he set out to create a KIPP school in Denver.

KIPP Sunshine Peak Academy (KSPA) opened in July 2002 with six teachers (four are TFA alums) and sixty students. In his role as the School Director, Rich has climbed a "massive learning curve." With the goal of getting his students to college, Rich operates his KIPP school on an intensive schedule. School runs from 7:25 to 5:00 every day, with half-days on Saturday for enrichment programs. The school year is longer—220 days versus the 180 required days for most districts. Students and parents must sign a commitment form upon enrollment, which lays out KSPA's structure of rewards, strong sense of discipline, and interaction between parent, teacher, and student. Rich Barrett commented on the school's success:

> A lot of schools say that they are creating a team environment, a family feeling. We are doing it. You can walk through the doors and see it, hear it, feel it. Our school looks like a home. It's an education home. Our students are excited to be here. We will continue to teach them in the best possible ways we know how.

Rich applied the lessons he gathered from TFA to KIPP Sunshine Peak Academy.

> I received the best training in Houston. It was wonderful. TFA provided me with support and resources beyond what I could have imagined. They never backed out of making me a better teacher and ultimately making my students more successful. I would do it all over again if I had the chance. Now I am working to take TFA's leadership model, the one they used to make an educator out of me, and apply that to KSPA in Denver.

Chris Barbic (1992, Houston) started his Teach For America career at Texas elementary school, which had previously been labeled as one of the worst schools in the state. He was discouraged to see his students leave elementary school and struggle against the obstacles of neighborhood secondary schools, in which illiteracy, drug abuse, teenage pregnancy, gang activity, crime, and high dropout rates prevented a culture of achievement. Chris wasn't alone in his concern; he joined with a group of frustrated teachers, students, and parents who met weekly to identify possible solutions. There simply wasn't a clear-cut solution that already existed, so the solution needed to be created.

The result was the 1995 creation Project Youth Engaged in Service (YES), a new middle school program that would be housed at his elementary school. Chris explained the logic behind the creation: "We realized: 'Why don't we just keep the kids here for middle school?'" In the following three years, 150 students were served at Project YES. Achievement was real and tangible; the daily attendance rate was 98% and students averaged a 90% passing rate on the Texas Assessment of Academic Skills (TAAS) test.

In 1998, Project YES had outgrown their space and viewed expansion as a future goal. Chris and his team applied for a state charter, moved to a new site, and expanded the program to include high school. Project YES, in fall 1998, opened its doors as YES College Preparatory School, a charter middle school with open enrollment for Houston middle and high school students.

Chris saw YES College Prep as a way to prove that "if you give kids from inner-city communities equal access and equal opportunity, they will do just as well as students from high-income schools." Of the three hundred yearly applicants, one hundred students are randomly selected from over forty zip codes. The goal is to graduate eighty-five students a year. YES College Prep measures a quality education in the skills and knowledge necessary to go to college. The bar is high. At YES, college is more than a goal; it is a graduation requirement. The school's charter mandates that each student receive a college acceptance letter to receive their diploma.

Hard work is at the crux of YES College Prep. Like KIPP, the school runs on an extended day from 7:50 to 5:00, and includes bimonthly Saturday school and an additional month of schooling in the summer. As a result, students spend 65% more time in school than their peers at regular public schools. With the willingness to do "whatever it takes," students, teachers, faculty, and parents sign the "Commitment to Excellence" which spells out clear expectations and goals. Enrichment activities include clubs, competitive team sports, and summer opportunities. There is an extensive Advanced Placement program, so that the average graduating senior has twelve A.P. credits to carry over to college. By the time they graduate, students have toured twenty-five colleges and universities on school field trips. The school culture, which is "strict with love," creates independence and self-sufficiency among students. The justification for every school decision is the "singular mission: Is this going to make our students ready for college?"

The results are phenomenal. In the 1999–2000 academic year, the YES high school was named the top-performing public high school in Texas based on attendance rates and standardized test scores. Out of approximately 180 Texas charter schools, YES College Prep is the only secondary school to receive an exemplary rating in the past three years. As far as results on the TAAS test, not only have YES students outscored students from neighboring inner-city schools, they have surpassed state averages. In 2002, 100% of YES College Prep's eighth graders passed the TAAS test, beating the state average of 86.5%. In 10th grade Math, 100% of YES students passed the TAAS, where the state average measures an 83% passing rate.

In June 2001, the first group of YES students graduated. All of the seventeen graduates continued on to college, securing letters of acceptance from Rice University, University of Texas, Stanford University, Cornell University, and Smith College. Two full-time college counselors assist students in the application process and guide students through finding scholarship money totaling $1.1 million. Eighty-five percent of those students are the first members of their families to attend college.

Chris attributed much of YES College Prep's mission, leadership, and foundation to Teach For America:

> TFA has been a great pipeline for great teachers. I hire Teach For America people because of their raw intelligence, their content knowledge, and their passion. Those are the things that engage kids and that make learning interesting for kids. Teach For America has given me the most profound learning opportunities of my life. I learned more through TFA and what resulted from it, than at any other stage of my life. It was nothing but a positive experience. It shaped the person I am now, what I value, and how I think about the world.

alums as school reformers

Other alums have worked to bring about educational reform in the private arena. In three years of teaching, Joel Rose (1992, Houston) came to believe that the public education system was broken. "I felt like I was a cog in a very broken wheel, and I wanted to fix that wheel. But I realized that it would take a new approach, thinking outside of the box to fix that wheel." His interest in educational reform took him to Edison Schools, a private company that partners with school districts and charter schools to assist in their management. When Edison opened in 1995, it managed four schools. The number grew to 136 schools.

> Usually what happens is a district will ask for help with a struggling school. These are traditionally schools in urban areas, with high numbers of students qualifying for free or reduced lunches, with histories of low performances in parent satisfaction and student motivation. They will come to us looking for a whole new philosophy, and they will pay our fee to implement our design.

Edison Schools are founded on ten fundamentals: schools organized for every student's success, a better use of time, a rich and challenging curriculum, teaching methods that motivate, assessments that provide accountability, a professional environment for teachers, technology for an information age, partnerships with families, schools tailored to their communities, and advantages of systems and scale. Edison schools pay particular attention to benchmark assessments. Students are tested monthly and results are aggregated, so that administrators and teachers can see and know what's happening in classrooms all the time. Students in grade three and above are given home computers; students and teachers communicate after school hours via e-mail and phone calls. Though Edison's success has been frequently refuted, Joel is confident in Edison's tremendous success; "If you were to look at the top fifty urban school districts and measure their rate of growth, Edison schools would be the highest performing district in terms of growth." Joel currently serves as Edison's Vice President for Client Services, responsible for overseeing student enrollment, financial reporting, site revenue projections, and company collection.

Joel looked to his Teach For America experience for providing an avenue into educational reform:

> I couldn't overstate how meaningful the experience was for me. For the past three summers, I have returned to Houston to see my fifth graders graduate. It's a remarkable experience to see who is graduating, who had dropped out, who has had a baby, who is in jail. Teach For America humanized educational issues. It's one thing to open up a newspaper and read about struggling schools. It's entirely different to know Michael, your fifth grade student who dropped out in eleventh grade to become an electrician.

In teaching first grade, Rowell Levy (1998, Phoenix) was startled by his discovery of "how much love I had for little kids." Another huge realization concerned the crucial involvement of parents in the classroom. Home visits gave him a better sense of where his students came from and enabled him to build community relationships. His effort to visit students' homes was fueled by his sense that "parents and teachers are working for the same thing. We are one team playing for the same goal." He joined with San Francisco School Volunteers, a non-profit organization that strives to get minority and new immigrant families more invested in their student's schools. Rowell helps schools create workshops to give parents tips on how to help their students with at-home reading and homework. Much of the focus is on immigrant parents as well as parents from low-income communities, who have historical traditions of minimal involvement and who have shown signs of benefitting the most from this involvement. San Francisco School Volunteers invites parents to school to participate in family book time, when classrooms are opened for parents to read with their children and to later reconvene for parent club meetings to discuss school policies and parenting experiences.

David Wakelyn (1990, Los Angeles) has always been animated by the question of what can be done to address the problem of low-performing schools. Three years of teaching in Inglewood, followed by research in failing schools, led him to believe that more money was a necessary, but not sufficient, approach to the questions. "The capacity to turn around low-performing schools can be built from within. Schools need to look internally at what can be done rather than pointing to external sources that they can't control."

A master's in public policy and a Ph.D. in education steered David to the Center on Education and the Economy (NCEE), a "think and do tank" focusing on standards-based reform. Their vision is that education and training are most effective with high standards for student achievement, accurate measurements of student progress, and solid instructional leadership through accountability. NCEE partners with both individual schools and districts, providing a model for comprehensive school reform. David, in his role focusing on data analysis, believes that "real school reform comes from making schools more coherent places to be." His work now pertains to integrating coherence and instructional leadership into low-performing schools. Though David is "proud to say that I was a part of Teach For America," he points out that "The real problem is not attracting top teachers, it's getting them to stay." He hopes that Teach For America will evolve as an organization, and consider other approaches to the problems of educational inequity.

alums as teacher educators

Michelle Rhee (1992, Baltimore) believes that her three years of teaching and a master's in public policy "solidified a commitment to public education, but I knew I wanted more of a systemic impact. I saw too many of my kids leave my classroom and lose what they had gained with less effective teachers." This frustration brought her to The New Teacher Project (TNTP), a non-profit group which partners with school districts and states to assist in recruitment, selection, training, and supporting excellent teachers.

Created in 1997, TNTP is a spin-off of Teach For America. By 1997, Teach For America had accumulated a wealth of knowledge about how to recruit, select, and prepare teachers for high needs schools. TFA founder Wendy Kopp hired Michelle Rhee to begin to shape the business model for TNTP. Though TFA and TNTP exist independently, there is much overlap between the two. TNTP relies very much on Teach For America's model of recruiting highly qualified teachers, though most TNTP applicants are career-switchers. The training process between the two organizations is based on the same fundamentals, and both programs are in line with a broader vision of closing the achievement gap for students in urban schools.

In its first year, The New Teacher Project entered into three contracts. After only five years, that number rose to twenty, with a client list made of school districts, universities, and state departments of education. In 2002, for every available position, TNTP received nine applications. Their clientele currently includes school districts in Los Angeles, Washington, D.C., New York City, Baltimore, and Atlanta. TNTP works with clients on all aspects of attracting and retaining new teachers—specifically recruitment, selection, training, placement, support, and certification. Michelle explained TNTP's mission:

Our goal is to find solutions for school districts to solve the crisis in urban education. One solvable piece of it concerns aggressive and strategic thinking about recruitment. Another is to ensure that the highest-achieving applicants will matriculate in school districts rather than be discouraged by the barriers of getting into teaching positions.

Since its launch, The New Teacher Project has attracted and prepared over six thousand candidates, with thirty-nine programs in nineteen states.

Teach For America has always been a constant in my life. It has been bittersweet to be in Baltimore for ten years, and to see people cycle through, leave, and in some cases return.
      —Amy Wilson (1992, Baltimore) on her transition from corps member to teacher educator

After five years in the classroom, Amy Wilson (1992, Baltimore) explored the field of traditional teacher education. With a master's in urban education, Amy came to the Johns Hopkins University as a teaching cohort coordinator. Not only does Amy teach education classes, she is responsible for supporting, advising, and observing teachers in their classrooms. Her work has kept her well connected to Teach For America, since almost 80% of Baltimore corps members complete their professional master's in teaching with the TFA–JHU partnership. Amy stated:

It seems like I can effect more change the more teachers I can help. So when I teach a group of teachers about how to use power writing in their classrooms, or how to systematically analyze the results of an assessment to decide where to reteach, indirectly, I could be having an influence on the learning of hundreds of kids. I think there is a dearth of educational professionals who have enough experience in urban schools to really know what is what when they stand up and talk about strategies to try in urban classrooms. The five years of experience that I have is not really so much, but it is so much more than the majority of my teacher education colleagues. I like that I am working from the inside to change perspectives about how people learn to teach and become successful at it.

These corps members and alumni are proof that Teach For America is more than a mere two-year commitment. In the words of Franklin County school superintendent Carl Harris, these alumni are reminders of "a piece that often gets lost in the debates surrounding Teach For America—the fact that many people stay past two years."

chapter nine

life after teach for america

The first ten years of Teach For America were about laying the seeds for long-term change to be brought about by this powerful alumni network. Those seeds are just beginning to grow and the blossoms are barely visible. What we need to see next is what those seeds will grow into. Teach For America instilled the idea that we, as alumni, need to forward opportunity for underserved children and districts. Over a lifetime, we could and had to make a difference. I know that it's not just me in this part of the battle, but I am joined by 10,000 alumni who have become catalysts. The questions we must now ask are, How can we put our power together? How can we take more deliberate action?

—Kim Jacobsen (1991, Los Angeles)

Upon leaving the classroom, alumni take on the second part of Teach For America's mission: to effect long-term change from a variety of professional fields. The following interviews reveal exactly how Teach For America alumni embark on powerful pathways to promote change from the arenas of politics, business, medicine, law, advocacy, social services, and policy. These alums are proof that leaving the classroom does not mean shedding Teach For America's commitment to social justice.

Wherever Teach For America alums go, two, three, five years down the road, a part of their thinking will always be influenced by their classroom experience.

—Rob Reich (1992, Houston)

politics

Bill Norbert (1990, New Orleans) transferred his feelings about social injustice to political action. Though Bill Norbert joined Teach For America's first ever charter corps with a hunch that "a great adventure was about to begin," he could never guess how his experience would lead him to the path of politics. "My classroom experience was positive, but also frustrating. I felt that I would be able to accomplish more for positive change in government," reasoned Bill.

Two years of teaching solidified Bill's commitment to "do something for education." He returned to his home state of Maine to pursue a law degree and to clerk for the State Supreme Court. In 1998, he threw his hat into the state legislature race and won on the Democratic ticket. His victory was rooted in the community relations that he learned as a teacher: knocking on doors, listening to citizens' concerns, and extending himself to the community. Bill currently serves as a state representative for Maine, specifically as the Majority Whip.

Bill found a natural progression from teaching to public advocacy:

I love the notion of public service. I enjoy finding common ground and building coalitions around issues and ideas. I enjoy fighting for the underdogs in our society who otherwise would have no voice in the process. The law can be the great equalizer for the disadvantaged. Public service is another very good way to effect change.

As a state legislator, educational reform is one of Bill's top priorities. He pointed out Maine's specific challenges in the educational realm:

Maine is the whitest state in the nation, but we're also very poor. We face challenges related to poverty. Additionally, we have an enormous geographic area to serve 1.3 million residents. That raises a battle among rural and urban school districts. We are always grappling with the questions of, Should we consolidate schools? How do we attract and pay quality teachers?

His focus is on reforming the school funding formula, to allow for more money to go to needy programs that focus on special education and English as a Second Language. Other policies include testing standards for children and teacher recruitment and credential requirements. The Maine state legislature is a teacher-friendly place, with almost a dozen current and former teachers holding seats in the House of Representatives. Fifty percent of Maine's state budget is devoted to public education. As a result of the statewide commitment to education, Maine has the highest high school graduation rate in the nation. Maine's seventh and eighth graders recently scored the nation's best math and reading scores. Bill hopes to increase Maine's historically low college attendance rates. In his final statement that "Education is the best investment we as a society can make," Bill exemplifies how alums have taken their classroom lessons and applied them to effect long-term change.

Bill Norbert is now serving his third term in office, as well as continuing his legal work as the executive director of the Maine Association of Criminal Defense Lawyers. He explains that despite the brevity of his experience, he constantly revisits the memories of his Teach For America experience: "It was a catalyst in my life. I will always remember how challenging Teach For America was, and also the energy and enthusiasm I felt. I'm always telling stories about it."

Julie Mikuta (1991, New Orleans) also entered the political arena, as an elected member on the Washington, D.C., Board of Education. In a landslide victory, Mikuta won 50% of the vote in a seven-way race. In June 2000, D.C., voters passed a referendum to reshape the Board of Education to increase its accountability; in its new form, five seats are held by elected members with four coming through mayoral appointment.

Though Julie was a rookie to the political arena, much of her professional experience pertained to educational reform. After her TFA commitment, Julie traveled to Oxford University, where she earned a master's in comparative education as a Rhodes Scholar. Upon returning to the States, Julie had a brief White House internship in domestic policy under Clinton. Next came two years of working for the SEED Public Charter School in D.C., as a teacher as well as the director of curriculum, technology, and teacher recruitment. She recently completed doctorate work in international education and joined the Teach For America staff as the Vice President of Alumni Affairs.

Julie credits much of her victory to a grassroots, door-to-door campaign supported by the energetic reform group called EdActionDC, comprised of fellow Teach For America alumni and other young education entrepreneurs. EdActionDC's members led the campaigning and fund-raising efforts and provided valuable political networking. With $16,000 in campaign donations, Julie distributed campaign literature to gain name recognition and received endorsements from local politicians, community leaders, and newspapers, including D.C. Mayor Anthony Williams and *The Washington Post*. Julie sees her victory as the proof that "everyday citizens can impact important issues that are on the bottom of ballots."

Julie will serve on the D.C. Board of Education for a four-year term, during which she also is the Co-Chair of the Committee on Teaching and Learning. She hopes the Board will redevelop standardized tests, question teacher qualifications, examine the needs of low-performing schools, and provide parents with students in low-performing schools with vouchers and supplemental enrichment services.

Julie revealed that her original commitment to Teach For America, because of its ideal of education as the great equalizer, carried her along her career path. Her work is far from done. "I loved teaching, but I didn't want to be limited to only one classroom. I wanted to fix the systemic issues that affect the classrooms across the country." In the road ahead, Julie hopes to address D.C.'s traditionally weak high schools, as well as continuing efforts toward professional development, strengthening community involvement, and increasing student achievement.

The opportunity to do concerted public service in areas of need brought Andrew Greenhill (1991, Houston) to three years of teaching and finally the larger political realm. In 1999, he became the campaign manager for Tucson mayoral candidate Robert Walkup. Running a victorious campaign, Andrew stayed on as Walkup's Chief of Staff:

> TFA showed me a side of institutions that I wasn't aware of before. I had learned about it in an abstract way, but I had very little connections in my own background to institutions with large bureaucracies. As a teacher, I learned how individuals can work within larger institutions.

Currently, Andrew focuses on "making the local government more effective and more efficient." Key issues for Andrew include parks and recreation, transportation, economic development, and homelessness. Andrew sees his work as "putting the public service component and the intellectual side together."

> My connection to the Teach For America mission is that I am very much drawn to activity that involves public service. The local government is not all that different than the bureaucracy of a school district. We face similar challenges: a lack of resources, a large bureaucracy, the question of institutional control. Whatever I do in life, the consistent thread will be both my desire to be a part of the community and to be able to give back as a public servant.

> *"Teach For America has made me committed to causes and working with the disenfranchised."*
>
> —Allison Serafin (2000, Houston)

public policy

After teaching for seven years in five schools, Allison Jack (1991, Los Angeles) left the classroom to pursue education policy. With a master's in public policy, Allison came to Chicago's Leadership for Quality Education as the Director of the Charter School Resource Center. A non-profit group founded in 1989, Leadership for Quality Education supports innovation in education, empowers new leaders to rethink schools, and partners with others to improve opportunities for children in Chicago Public Schools. Much of Allison's work focuses on new school creation through small schools and charter schools:

> Public schools today are too often built on a one-size-fits-all mentality. Charter schools tailor their programs and curriculum to populations that have been traditionally underserved. Charter schools bring resources to education that weren't there before, both in terms of monetary donations and the diversity and creativity they add. We, in Chicago, have charter schools that are linked to community-based organizations, to musical endeavors, and soon hopefully to museums.

Scott Joftus (1990, New York) uses a policy-oriented approach to address America's educational crisis. He hoped that a Teach For America experience would provide him with the chance to make a difference and to "shape the ideas I had about ways to get into education and youth policy." After completing his teaching commitment, Scott earned a master's in public policy from University of California at Berkeley. He later completed a doctorate in education policy and administration from the George Washington University. Next, Joftus began his career in national education policy, research, and evaluation. He currently serves as the Policy Director for the Alliance for Excellent Education, a newly formed advocacy organization based in Washington, D.C.

Alliance for Excellent Education aims "to have six million at-risk middle and high school students achieve high standards and graduate prepared for college and success in life." Specifically Scott works to shape policies based on research, to pull together studies, and to bring clarity to initiatives that ensure at-risk students receive an excellent education.

Currently Alliance for Excellent Education's primary goals are to put the following four initiatives into law and have them fully funded by the federal government: 1) create smaller schools, 2) provide tools to promote and engage adolescent literacy 3) ensure teacher and principal quality through professional development and 4) provide additional student support in after-school and summer school tutoring, counseling, and positive school environments. If the federal government adopts all four initiatives, the estimated cost will be $14 billion a year.

Scott came to Teach For America as an alternative route to a public policy career:

> I knew I wouldn't teach long term. The question was whether I would teach for two years, or three, or four. Ultimately I knew I would take more of a policy route. TFA gave me a real life understanding of the realities that I would later target through policy and advocacy. It was an invaluable opportunity to see firsthand the problems that public policy needs to address.

business

Though the correlation between business and education may be more subtle, alums like Kimberly Jacobsen (1991, Los Angeles) focus their efforts toward understanding how cost structures, financing, and budgeting affect schools. Kim entered her Compton classroom "not ever having thought about going into teaching." Her interest in Teach For America came from a combination of her travels in third world countries during college as well as working as a youth advisor in a Philadelphia high school, where graduation rates were only 25%. As a business and international relations major, Kim remarked, "It was easy to look at these underdeveloped countries and point out how education-

and policy-wise they weren't doing a good job. But during college I witnessed similar problems, in spite of the resources available in our country." Before pursuing a career in business and policy, Kim joined Teach For America to learn hands-on about the realities of underresourced areas, as well as the depth and complexity of the issues.

She came to Compton in 1991, when the district ranked at the bottom of California educational rankings and the threat of state takeovers loomed; "I saw teachers being blamed for the problems in education. I came to realize that the problems weren't because of a lack of passion, a lack of energy, or even a lack of ability." Since her commitment, Kim has earned simultaneous degrees at Stanford University: an MBA from Stanford's Graduate School of Business and a master's in education in learning, design, and technology from Stanford School of Education.

> Too often, teachers and principals are the scapegoats, when they are
> without access to tools to bring about systemic change. In the business
> world, we push tools and resources to the people who are closest to
> power. We need to translate this into education, so that teachers can be
> trained, mentored, and guided. Schools are designed in ways so that
> they cannot effect their own change.

Kim joined the Palo Alto, California, office of The Noyce Foundation, a non-profit organization dedicated to stimulating ideas and supporting initiatives to produce significant achievement for public school students in grades K–12. She serves as the Director of Product Development and Marketing. The Noyce Foundation's primary mission is restructuring schools and school systems. Although much focus is given to core academic subjects of math, literacy, and science, the Noyce Foundation hopes to give principals access to budget control as a means of reform. Kim credits Teach For America for providing an avenue into education, but "moreover, they gave me a powerful pathway to answer the question I had about what was a good place for me to focus my energy."

James Sparkman (1990, New York) has spent the years since his Teach For America commitment finding a way to bridge the worlds of business and education. In fact, the combination of entrepreneurship and the spirit of public service led James to Teach For America, when he served as one of the first-ever campus representatives for TFA's 1990 charter corps. After he graduated from Harvard Business School, his work remained in the education field—starting an educational loan program, founding a software company for colleges, and investing in education-related companies. At every stop along the way, James has felt tied to Teach For America's mission; "I am drawn to companies in the education arena 100% because of my TFA experience." James concluded that on the road ahead, he "might not stay in education as a business forever. But my political philosophies stem from those two years in the classroom. I know that regarding issues of social and public policy, I definitely draw on my TFA experience."

law

The desire to do meaningful work with populations in need led Matthew Lenaghan (1993, Houston) first to a Teach For America classroom and later to public interest law. After three years of teaching, he began law school and continued to teach law to high school students on the weekends. His next move, to Advocates for Children of New York, Inc. (AFC), seemed a natural step.

Established over thirty years ago, AFC represents New York City's most impoverished families to ensure quality public education services. The focus is on children up to age twenty-one who are at risk for academic failure brought on by school-based discrimination. Matthew provides direct representation to kids in New York classrooms, with 98% of his clients being students receiving special education services. AFC's clients include minorities, immigrants and English language learners, homeless children, and children living in foster care.

Much of Matthew's work involves contact with New York City schools and teachers. All students receiving special education services have an Individualized Education Plan (IEP), a legally binding document that lays out the program, services, and modifications that a student should receive. Matthew's practice involves seeing that Individualized Education Plans, legally binding documents that lay out the program, services, and modifications that a student should receive, are being upheld. When IEPs are inadequate or being violated, he fights for additional services or remedies. AFC provides a wide range of services for its clients, ranging from specialized tutoring or therapy to placement in other educational settings, both public and private.

Matthew was able to look back at his years teaching in Houston and admit both his own naivety and his school system's failure to uphold the law in the case of students with special needs. "I, never in three years of teaching, once saw an IEP. If someone had informed me about the law, I would have been concerned with my students' rights and the injustice of the situation. I would have addressed things differently." This feeling has prompted Matthew to offer his legal services to current Teach For America corps members, so that they can better understand legalities surrounding IEPs and special education students.

Matthew Lenaghan estimates that in four years with Advocates for Children of New York, he has served at least five hundred clients, and often their cases are ongoing. He believes "without reservation that teaching is more difficult, and more rewarding, than law school." In his field of public interest law, he states, "I am not changing the system, but I am dealing with one kid at a time. As in teaching, being able to say that some people are better off for having come in contact with me makes it worth it."

medicine

Charter corps member Sarah Van Orman (1990, Rural Georgia) joined Teach For America because of both her commitment to political activism and her interest in children and youth issues. She postponed her application to medical school and spent two years teaching high school in rural Georgia. After her commitment, Sarah remained convinced of her desire to pursue medicine, though her Teach For America experience led her to pursue it in a very different way:

> TFA made me realize that if you as a teacher, or as a physician, can help and inform people to make good, educated decisions about their futures, that that would be powerful responsibility indeed.

She earned her medical degree at Minnesota's Mayo Clinic and then completed her residency at the University of Chicago in a program combining internal medicine and pediatrics. Sarah points out that her interest in adolescent and young adult health comes largely from her classroom years. "I enjoyed taking care of people at that age, when they are at the cusp of forming who they will be in the precarious balance between childhood and adulthood." Sarah became the Medical Director for the University of Chicago's Student Health Services, and began a career of academic medicine, where she works both as a clinician and as an educator overseeing residents and medical students. Her desire to combine medicine and social services led to two years of work with Adopt-A-Pediatrician, in which pediatricians partnered with Chicago Public Schools. Once a week, physicians work at school sites through direct student involvement to promote health education and also with staff and parents to raise health awareness.

Not only did Teach For America lead Sarah to formulate the idea of working with adolescents, she credits it with improving her communication skills:

> One of the great experiences in my classroom was that sense that my students and I were so different that we were able to look at each other as coming from different cultures and different worlds. The reality is that in a diverse world, most people will work and live among people who are very unlike themselves. To be an effective physician, teacher, or most anything else, we must find ways to bridge cultural differences. Teach For America taught me the importance of cross-communicating

with people from other communities, the value of that, and how important it is to take care of each other.

Sarah speaks with a voice of advocacy in education:

As a person who has been in the classroom, it's important for me to speak out about the realities and challenges that students and teachers face as well as what it means to raise student achievement. Society has given me somewhat of a voice of authority because of my role as a physician, and I can use that voice to raise awareness about the importance of resources and school funding.

After leaving teaching to begin medical school, Jen Kerns (1996, Bay Area) revealed, "I miss teaching." Jen came to Teach For America with dual interests: becoming a teacher and becoming a doctor. "I couldn't reconcile between the two. Teach For America allowed me a structured teaching experience without having to spend additional years in a certification program." Her surprise was "how difficult, how emotional it was to leave the classroom after two years with the realistic knowledge that I might not come back to teaching."

Jen applies the lessons gathered in the classroom to her clinical rotations. "My classroom experience provided me with patience in working with people, a perspective in understanding people from different places." Teaching taught Jen compassion, understanding, and the importance of being non-judgmental, skills that are valuable in her current patient contact. "I learned more about learning, about communicating with others from my teaching experience than I learned in all of high school and college."

In fall 2002, Jen began her third year in a dual degree program with UC Berkeley and UC San Francisco. After five years, she will emerge with a medical degree as well as a master's in public health, and a master's in medical science. She has not left behind her interest in working with teenage girls, and thinks her field of interest is adolescent medicine, obstetrics, and gynecology, or family practice.

social services and advocacy

Many alumni follow a natural progression from the classroom to the world in non-profits, advocacy, and social services. Take, for example, Mina Kim (1998, New Jersey). Teach For America intrigued her because of its commitment to educational equity and because it allowed her to examine issues of gender equality; "I came to Teach For America because I believed I could make a difference and advance gender equality in the way I structured my classroom." Mina earned her teaching certificate and left the classroom to join Teach For America's regional office in Los Angeles as the Director of Operational Support. Mina's classroom experience deepened her commitment to empowering women and girls through meaningful educational opportunities.

However, Mina couldn't help but wonder about her students' futures after they left her first grade classroom:

> These kids had another eleven years of schooling. There were so many systemic or institutionalized obstacles for them to graduate high school. I wondered how many would get lost as they began to realize what and who they would have to compete with. It struck me that what I did may have had little value in the grand scheme of their lives. I felt far away and concerned in that I hadn't given them the tools that they would need to graduate from high school or go to college or fulfill the dreams they shared with me.

This conviction made Mina wonder if she could make a greater impact in another field, especially if it were integrated with her first passion for women's issues. In summer 2001, Mina joined Women and Youth Supporting Each Other (WYSE), as the organization's Executive Director. WYSE is a national mentoring organization in which college women are paired with middle school girls of color from low-income communities. Through a curriculum-based program, the organization empowers girls by providing them with the resources and support to make informed decisions about issues of identity like racism and sexism as well as women's health issues such as pregnancy and sexual decision-making issues. Since its 1992 inception, WYSE has trained seven hundred college women as mentors. Nine hundred girls have been provided the resources and support to make healthy, informed decisions and create community change through leadership roles. The program currently has eleven branches and selects mentors from the University of Chicago, Harvard, New York University, the University of California Berkeley, Yale School of Law, and several others. These college women go to nearby middle and high schools to provide their mentees with support through decision-making games, in-depth discussions, and community action. The result is a national network of support and friendship between college-age women and adolescent girls, with the goal of positive community change and self-betterment.

Laura Perkins (1999, Bay Area) credits her decision to pursue a master's in social work from Columbia University almost entirely to her teaching experience:

> I wouldn't have thought of this social work without Teach For America. I was so impressed seeing my students who did well, my students who persevered through such hardships. They were funny and smart and charming and amazing to be around. They were proof that some people could get through the system. It made me believe that anyone could do it, if they had the necessary supports in place.

Chris Myers (1994, Mississippi Delta) has remained in Sunflower County, Mississippi, since his original placement. After three years in the classroom, Chris became the Executive Director of the Sunflower County Freedom Project, an independent non-profit organization dedicated to educational excellence and leadership development. Students in the program sign a six-year commitment to excellence, agreeing to participate in intensive summer programs, classes every Saturday during the school year, study sessions after school, and martial arts training.

Chris created the program to bridge the gap between elementary and high school. As a fifth grade teacher, Chris witnessed his students go on to middle school and "get off track." Chris explains, "We give our students academic support and cultural experiences to help them stay in school and to inspire them to go on to college." The goal of the program is to create a well-rounded student who is academically capable, socially conscious, and mentally disciplined. Though some of the program is funded by grants and private contributions, students are expected to pay a fraction of their costs.

> This principle came mostly from parent feedback and our Board of Directors. Parents were frustrated by this pernicious, pervasive attitude of getting something for nothing. Our students grow up in communities where they get free lunches and their parents collect welfare money. We want to discourage the idea that kids don't have to work in order to get something. We create a connection between work and rewards.

Much is expected of the sixty students in the program. During the school year, they spend every night in a two-hour study hall and in martial arts classes, which complement the academic program's self-discipline and goal-setting. There are additional classes on Saturday mornings, and for six weeks in the summer, students enroll in an intensive summer program held at the University of Mississippi. Here students spend their days in reading, writing, and math classes, and they attend a drama program in the evening. The summer program culminates in a trip. Younger students spend eight days traveling through Southern cities connected to civil rights history, including Selma, Birmingham, and Montgomery. Older students travel to Washington, D.C., and New York, visiting colleges and universities along the way. "These trips expose our students to the world beyond the Delta. They see what education can do for them and their futures. Education is the freedom to do what they want."

Chris pointed to his Teach For America background as the means to where he is today.

> For me, Teach For America did what it promises to do. TFA took a kid from a top college who otherwise wouldn't have set foot in the field of education. They trained me well enough to get me started. They put

the ball in my hands and told me to go with it. TFA alums need to move beyond the two-year commitment and take their experience to make a lasting change. Making long-term changes in the communities we serve is how real change happens.

The Teach For America experience provided Kara Forte (1992, Los Angeles) with the realization that "schools alone can't handle the problems our children face. Our students need a comprehensive experience to make it through high school and on to college." Kara pursued both a master's in multicultural education and a doctorate in the politics of education. Believing that inner city populations are "treated with no value," Kara became the Director for the New York office of the "I Have a Dream" Foundation.

The "I Have a Dream" Program helps children from low-income areas reach their education and career goals by providing a long-term program of mentoring, tutoring, and enrichment. To start each project, the program adopts an entire grade from an elementary school or an entire age group from a public housing development. They work with the group of children—"the dreamers"—and their families year-round, following them from elementary school through to college. Services provided to the dreamers include mentoring, homework help, summer programs, field trips, and other enrichment activities, including karate, dance and voice lessons, and arts and crafts. Not only do children benefit, but so do their parents. The Dreamers' parents receive parenting classes, GED classes, computer training, and job placement services. Dreamers are always welcome at drop-in centers. The foundation strives to build long-term trusting relationships to provide students with a role model who takes a vested interest in them. Research points out that Dreamers have better school attendance, less involvement with juvenile justice, resistance to peer groups and peer pressure, higher graduation rates, improved grades and test scores, higher educational aspirations, and improved college attendance.

"I Have a Dream" hopes to enable its participants to become productive citizens, who graduate high school and are prepared for college and careers beyond. The first group of Dreamers graduated in 1981. Without support, it was typical for 10% of a representative population to graduate high school. Ninety percent of the first-ever Dreamers graduated from high school. Sixty percent of the same group continued on to graduate from college. "I Have a Dream" guarantees its graduates tuition for state schools and links students to a variety of sponsors for financial assistance.

Kara believes that "Teach For America made me who I am today." Her teaching experience gave her a huge sense of accomplishment in her own capabilities, but also fueled her vision of a more equal society. She remains "passionate about the need for solutions to solve the crisis that the U.S. is a stratified society."

Teaching in the South Bronx left Janna Wagner (1995, New York) with the frustrating reality that "I got to my kids in third grade too late. Society had already given up on these thirty-two children and they were only in third grade." Janna drew the conclusion that "we need to catch children younger." After earning a master's in education from Harvard Graduate School, Janna joined up with a friend to co-found All Our Kin, an early childhood education collaborative based in New Haven, Connecticut.

All Our Kin allows single parents on public assistance to meet their job training and work participation requirements by working with their own children in an on-site lab school. Parents train to become professional early childhood educators, who graduate from the nine-month program ready to establish their own family day cares or to work in existing day care centers.

The program arose in response to changes in welfare laws, which created a mandated work component as well as limiting recipients to a maximum time limit of five years. Janna's work in the South Bronx left an indelible sense that "low-income people don't have choices about their lives. They have to decide between work or their families." All Our Kin provides childcare while creating excellent teachers and future leaders who will use their childcare expertise not only for their own children, but for their larger communities as well. All Our Kin assists graduates in finding jobs at high-quality child care centers or in setting up family child care in their neighborhoods. Janna explained, "We work hard to ensure our participants graduate with enough skills, knowledge, professionalism and commitment to get excellent jobs in top-notch centers in New Haven."

All Our Kin selects and trains intelligent, creative, and loving women who may lack academic credentials because they had babies at young ages. Women attend classes from 9 to 3 and over the course of the year-long commitment receive five hundred hours of hands-on instruction and two hundred hours of classroom time. Women receive job readiness preparation as well as computer literacy skills. The children of these women also benefit from increased school readiness, early literacy, and social skills to prepare them for academic success. Since its 1999 creation, All Our Kin has served approximately six to twelve women a year and their children.

According to Janna, "All Our Kin uses education to dismantle poverty. The welfare population isn't what most people assume it to be. To move people out of poverty, society has to reimagine this population, invest in them, in their futures, and in their education." Janna credits Teach For America with helping to form her commitment to public service and social justice.

> For me, teaching is activism. Teaching is about building relationships with communities, challenging inequity, fighting for social justice, and making change for all Americans. Teach For America helped support my commitment to becoming a catalyst for change in my community. I have always been a "doer"—someone who dreams of something better and works to get there. Teaching allows me to take the anger that I have about injustice, focus it, and make a difference every day.

communication

Teach For America took Seth Kugel (1992, New York) to a bilingual classroom in a Bronx elementary school where the majority of students came from immigrant families of the Dominican Republic. What emerged was insatiable curiousness about immigration policy and the issues that Latino immigrants in the Bronx faced. In the classroom, Seth's students began a unit on immigration, where they interviewed and wrote biographies of family members who were living the immigrant experience. Seth recalled, "The common themes that resulted from their work—the idea of adjusting to life here, the idea of trans-nationalism (people living in two countries simultaneously), the fascination immigrants had with their homelands—were the most fascinating subjects I had ever looked at. I remember thinking, 'I could really study this.'" Seth began to think about immigrant issues, first on a trip with a student's family to the Dominican Republic. His fascination turned to more formal study at Harvard's Kennedy School of Government, where Seth focused on immigration policy. Next he turned to working for four years for the New York city government in social service agencies.

What emerged was a natural progression to freelance writing. Seth currently freelances his writing to the City Section of *The New York Times*, in addition to teaching journalism classes at New York University. His writing career stemmed directly from his Teach For America experience; "Teach For America made me reassess what the immigrant experience meant." Through his articles, Seth paints an accurate portrayal of what is going on in the lives of immigrant children. Recent articles have focused on the efforts of Dominicans in Upper Manhattan to vote in their homeland elections and the ritual of airline flights between New York and the Dominican Republic. In addition to covering the Bronx, a common theme which Seth addresses is the cultural conflicts that pervade the lives of immigrants. He writes to "expose and describe a sector of life in New York City that is not often written about."

Seth applies the social skills that he acquired as a teacher to his current work in journalism:

> My number one tool is my Spanish. My number two tool is to always accept invitations into the community—be it dinner at a student's

house or a trip with a student's family to the Dominican Republic. I always read Spanish books and newspapers and listen to Spanish music. It's a sort of immersion. If I spent enough time in the environment, I would learn how to behave and interact in a community different than my own. My own acceptance, as a teacher and as a journalist, happened very naturally but because of a lot of work.

Anina Robb (1996, New York) writes in a very different genre, though she sees her work as still connected to Teach For America's mission. Anina came to Teach For America with prior work experience in writing and text book publishing. She was shocked to discover that textbooks were being written by people who had little or no classroom experience. In her South Bronx classroom, Anina translated her own passion for writing to meaningful instruction. She created a literary magazine in her school. She could not, however, shake her frustration about the lack of resources in low-income areas. "Not only were there almost no books for my students, it was difficult to find materials that were high-interest level but could be read by my students who weren't reading at grade level." With a master's in writing, Anina focused on writing professional books and resources for struggling middle-school readers. "The materials I am writing now target teachers who are working with the same content and grade-level that I taught. Hopefully these resources will get into the hands of teachers who can help middle-schoolers learn to read and write."

Anina came to Teach For America because it provided a side door into the complicated New York City school system. The overwhelming systemic bureaucracy led to her decision to leave teaching:

> Toward the end, I felt totally overwhelmed by the system. I didn't have it in me to make changes politically by going into the system. It was too big of a machine to even look at. Yet my experience was meaningful and I didn't want to leave education. I wanted to continue to contribute.

She now combines writing and education through part-time teaching and writing educational materials for Scholastic and Houghton Mifflin.

Molly Blank (1998, Washington, D.C.) emerged from the classroom with the desire to spread the word of the inequities she had witnessed. Growing up in a politically liberal family, she believed her place in the world was to help. After two years of teaching fifth grade, Molly left the classroom:

> The decision to leave was not easy at all, but it was what I needed to do. Teaching was so hard. I internalized a lot. I had such a high level of stress. I took everything so personally. But at the same time, I loved my kids and there was much about teaching that I loved. There were moments when things were so good, but I knew ultimately that the classroom wasn't where I would be happy in the future.

She left to begin a career in documentary films, primarily films about social change and nonviolent action. After teaching, Molly began writing a documentary film about educational inequity in the nation's capital. According to Molly, the decision to join Teach For America and her current work as a master's in journalism student at UC Berkeley very much go hand-in-hand; "I am pursuing my interest in documentary films with stories of injustice to tell. I know I will pursue this for the same reasons I joined Teach For America."

Finally, in her current position as the Vice President of Teach For America Alumni Affairs, Julie Mikuta (1991, New Orleans) explained the ongoing mission of the alumni network.

> Educational equity will only happen when there is a confluence of events triggered from all arenas of society, not only the voice of educators but the voices of those in law and business and medicine. Real systemic change can only happen when all of these professionals finally send a unanimous message that this is a priority, that we can make it happen, and here are the resources to make it happen. Our alums have

seen firsthand what the problems are and what the solutions are. It is their responsibility to demand that we raise the standards societal-wide and demand more for the kids of our nation. There are many ways to go about effecting long-term change. There's a civic piece to educate yourself when you go to the polls. We need to demand that our policy makers, from the bottom of the ballot all the way up, make good education decisions. There's dispelling the myths. Educate the people around you—friends, family, neighbors—to fight the stereotypes that surround inner-city students and schools. We need to encourage proactivity in communities.

chapter ten

the more you teach, the more you learn

Teach For America was the toughest job I'll ever love.
　　　　　　　　　　　　　　　　—Jason Levy (1993, Houston)

It's an emotional roller coaster. It's humbling and wonderful.
It's the first real time in my life that I have ever been really challenged.
I hate it and love it all at the same time.
　　　　　　　　　　—Danielle DeLancey (2002, North Carolina)

One of the last stages in the Teach For America journey is the reflection that comes at the end of a school year or at the end of the two-year commitment. Corps members speak of a wide range of emotions, of a life-changing experience, of a new consciousness, and of sobering realizations. They credit Teach For America and their students with exposing them to realities, with helping them to discover voices of advocacy, and with shaping their outlooks and future paths. Here corps members look back on what they have gained from their classroom years, often discovering that teaching and learning occur simultaneously.

eye-opening realities

Emily Glasgow (1998, Bay Area) was placed in one of Oakland's most troubled elementary schools, where three principals came and left in the course of two years, where eight year olds faced pervasive urban violence, and where third graders came to school several levels behind grade level. She spent two years teaching in a run-down classroom with no air conditioning, no carpet, and no ventilation. An intensely over-crowded school with twelve hundred students, it had no grass and no play structure. Amongst those challenges, Emily found sources of inspiration in dynamic teachers and children with "strong personalities and amazing characters."

In reflecting upon her placement, Emily concluded the following:

> Teach For America was my window into something I wouldn't other-wise have had. I got a broader perspective on the world, on cultures so different than my own. I've become aware of larger levels of poverty and social issues. I've gotten new perspectives on urban realities. I've gotten new perspectives on systems in our country, how they work, how they don't work, who makes the decisions, and whom those deci-sions affect. I've realized that change can happen, no matter how grad-ual it is.

That sense of awareness stretched Emily to advocate for her students and their communities. She learned to assert her voice of advocacy to promote change:

> I learned how to stand up and fight for my kids. I've learned not to take no for an answer and to fight until my kids get what they need. I've learned to become comfortable in a culture and community so dif-ferent than my own.

Additionally Emily learned to work within communities, in which she originally felt as an outsider. "I have stopped perceiving myself as an outsider and become comfortable with daily interactions, home visits."

In fall 2000, Emily opened a small school in Oakland, California. She left Oakland to pursue a master's in education and a principal's certificate from Harvard's Graduate School of Education.

real-life understanding

For charter corps member Kelly Amis (1990, Los Angeles), Teach For America gave faces to poverty and racism through knowing her students and their communities. Kelly came to Teach For America with a love of working with students. In her first year, Kelly taught over thirty fourth and fifth grade students in South Central Los Angeles. "When I came to Teach For America, I didn't expect to continue teaching. But I was astonished and dismayed by what I saw." She watched her new city erupt in racial strife as the 1991 Los Angeles riots tore her community and her students apart. School closed as looters destroyed neighborhoods and buildings smoldered. Four days later, she returned to school aware of the presence of the National Guard. "It was unlike anything you'd ever think you'd see in America. People were held hostage in their own homes and neighborhoods."

Kelly watched students at both ends of the spectrum, who embodied both despair and hope. She remembered her fourth grader Deshaun, who was functionally illiterate. As Kelly began to understand the life challenges Deshaun faced—only being able to write his first name, his home life of drug addiction and signs of abuse—she sensed that he had already been written off by a school system incapable of providing him with the intervention he needed. For Kelly, Deshaun was one of too many lost or forgotten students. And yet, Kelly remembered her student José, the son of low-income immigrant parents. In spite of the challenges, José relied on his innate intelligence and his drive to get into a magnet high school. He traveled two hours each way on public transportation to get to and from high school. To pay his way through college, he joined the army. Kelly saw José as a miracle. "He epitomized the children in public schools who have to do so much just to get a fighting chance."

Kelly emerged from her classroom experience knowing that Teach For America expanded her universe. "It gave me a real life understanding of what it means to be poor, what it means to live in the inner city." She carried those lessons with her in her current career path, in her continued mentoring of students, and in her politics and thinking. "I always refer to my experience with TFA. It made me a person who doesn't so much see "us" versus "them." Teach For America started her lifelong commitment to social justice and educational reform. Kelly pursued a master's in education policy analysis from Stanford University.

> I realized that I could have a larger impact, more influence on our nation's poorest children through educational policy. Though I left teaching per se, I remain committed to Teach For America's mission. That's how important it is to me—it's a mission, not a job.

Upon earning her policy degree, Kelly became a Fulbright scholar and traveled to Australia to study their education system. She landed her current job with a Washington, D.C.,–based non-profit organization, Fight For Children. The mission of Fight For Children mirrors that of Teach For America: to improve the quality of life for children and families in need.

> I stayed involved in the mission because of the pervasive injustice that kids experience not only day after day, but decade after decade. When we think about our nation's poorest schools, people lose their shock value. But it amazes me—even after all these years of being so rooted in the problem—that in the wealthiest nation in the world we have schools that cannot even teach the most basic literacy skills.

With Fight For Children, Kelly works closely with teachers and school communities to bring about educational reform. Kelly points to Teach For America for her introduction to her current line of work:

I have huge respect for this program, for this mission. Teach For America takes people like me, who may have otherwise pursued very different routes in life, and makes them into educational reformers for life. It changes people's perspective on things and gets them passionate about improving things.

a voice of advocacy

With these acquired understandings of the realities of low-income communities, corps members become advocates for their students and students' families. Teach For America gave Scot Fishman (1997, Washington, D.C.) the following:

> I gained the power to advocate for my students. When I'm among doctors and businessmen and attorneys, I will be able to shed light upon areas and realities that they have not seen. Eventually their eyes will be opened.

In his final year of law school at the University of Virginia, Scot continues to talk about his Teach For America experience, in recruiting undergrads and in carrying his advocacy with him to the legal profession. He continues to mentor two of his former students, tenth grader Timothy and eighth grader Thedro, who have grown up with minimal male leadership.

Melea Bollman (1998, Rio Grande Valley) didn't come to Teach For America thinking that she'd stay in teaching. She found, however, that teaching gave her the awesome ability to reach her students; "It was challenging. I was in a powerful position to effect change and to impact the futures of my students." The challenges of teaching in a South Texas behavior modification classroom led her to the following conclusion:

> Teach For America made me a strong advocate for at-risk children. It made me realize that all students can achieve academic success, and that success is empowering to them as well as it was to me.

Melea worked as a Program Director for Teach For America in the Bay Area and believes that Teach For America "solidified my commitment for working with at-risk students for the rest of my life." She currently teaches special education students in Key West, Florida.

the power of teaching

As a first-year teacher, Maureen Kay (1999, Washington, D.C.) arrived as "an idealist, an eternal optimist, and full of excitement and energy." Her enthusiasm was evident in her collaboration with the University of Maryland's Mid-Atlantic Regions Japan in School (MARJiS) grant. She took classes focused on international education, primarily Japanese culture and its school system. Maureen applied that knowledge to infuse Japanese into the curriculum for her second and third graders. Her school paired with a Japanese school to form a pen pal alliance and video conferencing; "My kids got to know kids from a whole other world and what that world looked like." After two years, MARJiS sent Maureen on a six-week summer trip to Japan, in which she observed schools, studied the culture, and participated in a home-stay. In noticing immediate cultural and educational differences, Maureen questioned American societal realities at a deeper level:

> In Japan, there was amazing educational equity. I visited a very poor school outside of Tokyo and they had brand new music equipment and microscopes. In Japan, I was so jealous of how student-centered schools were, how respected teachers were, and how valued children were. The MARJiS partnership fueled my interest in working to resolve the glaring inequities we face.

In fall 2002, Maureen began graduate work at Harvard's Graduate School of Education, focusing on urban education policy and international and comparative education. She was surprised to find the following:

> The more I learn about the policy world and the political game, the

more I understand the power of teaching. Inevitably I feel I'll be back in the classroom to make change at a more direct level.

Maureen attributed her current career path entirely to her Teach For America experience:

> There's no turning back once you become involved with TFA. I was exposed to so many social ills. I came face to face with discrimination and poverty. You can't help but become a lifelong advocator. To call myself a teacher is Teach For America's responsibility.

lessons from students

Though corps members are placed in the toughest schools and districts, rare is the corps member who will disparage their students. Rather than extend the difficulty of their work to their students, corps members come away amazed by the drive, perseverance, and resilience of their students. Jonas Zuckerman (1991, Bay Area) struggled though inconsistent classroom management and floundered to figure out the best way to teach his fifth graders. In a school deeply entrenched in poverty, students sat in classrooms without heat and played on a buckling school yard without gym equipment. Within two weeks of his first year, Jonas knew that he wanted to spend the rest of his life teaching. He explained, "I loved the kids. I loved the interactions. I loved being a part of the school community." He witnessed the diligence and resolve of his third grade student Timmy:

> One day we went on a field trip to the Museum of Children's Art. Timmy didn't come to school, but he showed up at the museum by himself at 11:15. He hadn't wanted to miss the learning, so he got himself on a city bus and found his way to where we were. He was only eight years old.

Jonas spent nine years teaching at his original placement and then switched to teaching at an Oakland high school, where he had an exceptional experience: teaching some of his first class of students, who were then in high school. In observing the range of inequity that students face, Jonas stated:

> I'm in awe of kids who graduate from high school. Sometimes even the mere fact that these kids show up everyday is simply remarkable. They demonstrate amazing resiliency.

solidified commitments

Teach For America changed me. It gave me a reality check on who I am. My idealism was not washed away, but it was hardened.
—Derek Redwine (1995, Houston)

Heather Graham (1993, New York) joined Teach For America to have an impact on school reform. She built trusting relationships with students and their families and believed "that I could learn from them as much as they could learn from me." She established extracurricular clubs and relied on incentives to reward students for academic effort and good behavior. She credits Teach For America with creating lasting relationships, like that with her fifth grade student Joel. Immediately Heather recognized Joel's artistic talent and worked to bring up his confidence level. Over the next eight years, Heather kept in touch with Joel, via letters and e-mail. When Joel was accepted into a magnet arts high school, Heather sent him books to prepare for the SATs and spoke with him about college. She remembers when Joel called her and said, "I want you to know that my high school graduation is in two days. I have a ticket for you." Joel won a scholarship to study visual arts at a New York City college and told Heather, "You pushed me. It wouldn't have happened without you."

The chance to work with students like Joel solidified Heather's commitment to educational equity and reform, social justice, and community development. After Teach For America, Heather traveled to Asia with the Henry Luce Scholars Program, where she studied educational policy in provincial China. She earned a Master's in public policy from the Woodrow Wilson School at Princeton University and studied the impact of small business loans on disadvantaged students in Peru. With the Annie Casey Foundation, Heather worked on education reform and community development for three years. Heather is currently a White House Fellow, having earned a highly competitive one-year non-partisan fellowship. She works at the USA Freedom Corps, a White House office launched in 2002 by President Bush to promote a culture of service, citizenship, and responsibility by expanding volunteer opportunities. Heather concludes, "Teach For America was the catalyst to my continued commitment to education reform and youth achievement."

a healthy dose of humility

The experience of a new culture and being thrust into the classroom was so humbling. This humility was a way of maturity and growing up. I learned to keep my mind open all the time. I was in charge of learning, but I had to admit that I didn't know all of the answers all of the time.
—Matthew Schmitt (1999, New Orleans)

John Keisler (2000, New Jersey) found that the educational crisis had deep roots in his Newark middle school. In the past decades, the state of New Jersey has taken over thirty statewide school districts and the Board of Education budget gap has measured as much as $80 million. John's school was ranked second to last in the district based on statewide test results. He saw signs of urban strife and economic turmoil at school. Students lived in local housing projects, where they faced the burdens of drug abuse, physical and sexual abuse, lead poisoning, and Fetal Alcohol Syndrome. "It felt like third world conditions," stated John. One hundred percent of students qualified for reduced-price or free lunches, and many more received dinner at after-school programs.

As a young white teacher, John felt ostracized by many of his colleagues:

> During my first year, I was the only white teacher who taught grades six
> through eight. I was later told that other teachers tried to have me fired
> on the premise that I wasn't qualified to teach black students. I had
> been accused of trying to brainwash black children and that I should
> "stop teaching my bourgeois ethics." Teachers admitted to having placed
> bets that I'd leave within my first two months. That teacher lost $10.

He worked diligently to find resources, often paying for them out of his own pocket.

> If you knew the right people—janitors and secretaries—you might have
> a chance at getting the right books and new supplies. For the most part,
> I was on my own for supplies. It wasn't that there was no funding. It
> was that money wasn't used correctly.

Of nearly six hundred students, there were a disproportionate number of students with special needs.

> We were a dumping-ground school. Other schools would dump their
> problems into low-performing schools, like mine. As a result, all of our
> special needs classes were overfilled. The state mandates a ratio of one
> certified teacher to every eight special needs students. At my school,
> there were usually twelve students in a class—often times far more.

The high number of students with special needs had ramifications on the larger school environment as well. "With such overcrowding, it forced students with special needs into mainstream classrooms, where their needs weren't met." In his first months in the classroom, John gave his seventh grade students a diagnostic reading comprehension test. Of the fifteen tested, nine read at or below a third grade level. "It's not that our students couldn't read. It's that they couldn't understand

what it meant. The children were not taught to think."
    Both students and teachers suffered with such bleak obstacles.

> The majority of kids admitted that they didn't feel safe coming to
> school. They felt that most of the time, teachers didn't have the control
> to enforce rules. Many teachers were pessimistic about the school sys-
> tem, as well, for lack of district support. Many teachers felt there was
> little they could do about behavior problems.

On top of the grim realities of his school and his city, John dealt with
the personal and social challenges of relocation to a new city without
the comforts of home or loved ones.

> It was overwhelming to attack the whole thing at once. You have to
> wake up every morning and decide what your goal is for that day. That
> motivates you to get up and go. I was coming to terms not with how
> the world should be or could be, but rather this is how the world is.

In his third year at his original placement, John reflected on the sense
of humility he gained through teaching.

> It's tremendous that someone has entrusted me with a year of a child's life.
> I will always have experiential knowledge to take with me. I finally began
> making progress when I began to let go. As overachievers, TFA teachers
> are forced to do something they have never had to do before—let go. I
> was humbled. It is a paradigm shift to stop looking at yourself as the one
> making the change, and then to simply become a part of the change.

transforming identities

> *Teach For America defined everything about who I am. During those
> two intense years, I grew the most, learned the most. The experience
> gave me the belief that I could do anything. More importantly, Teach*

For America began my lifelong commitment to education. How could it not? You can't see those realities, that injustice and not want to work towards bringing about change.
                    —Melissa Dyckes Storm (1994, Southern Louisiana)

Adam Mitchell (1999, Bay Area) is convinced that he would not be where he is in life now without Teach For America. After three years of teaching in East Palo Alto's Ravenswood District, he found himself in the middle of the political arena. His political involvement first began through negotiating a contract between the teachers' union and the school board. In protests, rallies, and community events to represent teachers' interests, Adam was discouraged to find that the union and its individual teachers were treated with "disdain." He realized that "nothing would change until the school board was replaced by new, responsive members."

Troubles with the school board coincided with district-wide turmoil. The Ravenswood District fought a lawsuit regarding the rights of special education students, draining money at a rate of $500,000 per month. The possibility of a state takeover loomed. With an impending school board election, Adam set his sights on winning a school board seat. He resigned from his full-time teaching position to run for the school board. It wasn't enough to win one seat; to make significant change, Adam and his supporters from the Coalition for Quality Education wanted to control the school board by winning three total seats. They ran a coordinated campaign, which was bolstered by community supporters and volunteers. Adam and his campaign supporters knocked on doors, worked phone banks, manned polling places, walked through neighborhoods, and posted flyers, posters, and door hangers. On November 5, 2002, Adam and his colleagues won and took control of the Ravenswood School Board. Adam attributed his victory to "outworking the incumbents, overwhelming the community with our message, and running an entirely positive campaign without relying on mudslinging tactics." Adam saw the landslide victory and his subsequent nomination of President of the Board as "a resounding win, a mandate that we needed to promote change."

In addition to his Board position, Adam runs the grants program for the San Francisco Education Fund. He oversees $155,000 in grants to support professional development and teacher leadership. His focus now is on the rebuilding phase, an eighteen-month plan to bring in a top-notch educator to serve as the district superintendent. For the diverse population of five thousand students in the Ravenswood District, he strives toward building an excellent urban district which will achieve outstanding results.

> *On the last day of school, we were cleaning up the room, taking posters down from the walls. One particular student walked up to me and said "Mr. Ables, I want to thank you. The whole year you never yelled at us. You never told us to shut up. You never called us stupid. We appreciate that." It broke my heart to hear this, but I remember that instance more than anything else. If I did nothing else for these students, they felt safe and cared for in my classroom.*
>
> —David Ables (1997, Bay Area)

Gary Rubinstein (1991, Houston) believes that Teach For America made him a better person, a more caring individual, and a more responsible adult. He links his identity inextricably to Teach For America and teaching:

> My entire identity now is as a teacher. If I were to die now, my tombstone would read "Teacher." Teaching is the thing that I've done to make a difference in this world. Over the years, I've taught a couple thousand kids. It amazes me that there are two thousand people out there that regard me as their teacher. Teach For America is the best decision I've ever made.

After four years of teaching in Houston, Gary was awarded Teacher of the Year for Houston Independent School District. In his fourth year of teaching, he volunteered to teach the standardized review class, which included seniors who were retained for failing the math section of the TAAS test—Texas's high-stakes test. Some of the students had failed as many as five times and would not graduate until they earned passing scores. At the end of the year, twenty-four of twenty-five students passed the test and earned their high school diplomas. Gary pursued a master's in computer science and moved to New York, where he currently is involved in teacher training with the New York Teaching Fellows project. After September 11, Gary came out of a five-year teaching retirement to take over a vacated position at Stuyvesant High School, only blocks from Ground Zero. In a life entirely focused on education, Gary continues to work as a private tutor, a teacher trainer, and offers workshops for new teachers.

> *Teach For America opened up my heart to learn to serve for others. Teaching isn't about how good of a teacher I am; what really matters is how my students, and how I, grow as human beings and as intellectuals.*
> —Anne Sung (2000, Rio Grande Valley)

the mission continues

> *I look at the fight for educational equity as a civil rights issue. It's not a mere two-year commitment. It's a mission. We are supposed to be taking our experiences and becoming advocates.*
> —John Keisler (2000, New Jersey)

Like many Teach For America corps members, David Silver (1995, Los Angeles) joined not knowing whether he'd ultimately wind up as a lifelong educator. And like many corps members, he struggled in his first year with classroom management in an overcrowded bilingual classroom. His sensational energy and charisma were contagious for his students, their families, and the Teach For America corps members who looked to David for leadership. His commitment to educational equity has far exceeded two years, and he is a lifelong educator, school leader, and veteran on the front lines of educational reform.

In two years of teaching in Compton and a third in Oakland, David coached his elementary school's basketball team, led parent workshops, visited colleges with his students, and made significant literacy gains with his students. From 1998 to 2000, David worked as TFA Program Director of the Bay Area corps. Not only did he strengthen the corps morale, he provided incoming corps members with tangible support and professional development opportunities. In 1999 and 2000, he joined the Teach For America summer institute staff as a school director. He pursued a principal's credential and a master's in administration from Harvard's Graduate School of Education, where he delivered the 2001 commencement speech. From 2001–2002, David served as a rotary scholar in Mexico, where he visited the extended families of fifteen of his former students, strengthened his Spanish, and worked with families and other educators to develop a vision for a new school, Think College Now, in Oakland.

Think College Now emerged from David's observation that students' families were interested, but often lacked the capacity for their children to attend college. With the help of parents, students, community members, and educators, David's proposal to develop his ideas into a new school was approved by the Oakland Unified School District. Think College Now focuses on ensuring more urban students have access to college. The school program includes early college exposure, a strong focus on student achievement, parent relationships, and community partnerships. To make college a reality, the school focuses on literacy gains of 1.5 grade levels per year and principles of respect, reflection, and resiliency. David shared his passion in a speech given to the 1999 Oakland corps members:

> And it will get better in our schools . . . we have no choice. In our schools, our work is not done. Until all of our kids have an equal shot, we will not stop. Whether it be in or out of the classroom. Until our

kids have the same amount of materials, we will not stop. Until our kids have the same chance to go to college, we will not stop. Until all of our students have the dignity of opportunity and excellence, we will not stop. The challenge of our lives is to do more than not forget, but also to act. We must continue to find creative ways to impact our students, our communities, and educational equity. Action is in my blood, in your blood. This is what Teach For America has given me.

the hope in tomorrow

I still have hope for public education. I've seen both ends of the spectrum now. Where I grew up, perhaps there were more resources and more tangible successes. But at the opposite end of the spectrum, where I taught with Teach For America, there is so much energy, so much promise. There are choices, there are improvements, and there are incredible things going on.

—Emily Glasgow (1998)

By its very nature, teaching is an act of hope, optimism, and investing in the future. Corps members may find that the current realities of our nation's public schools may be austere, but the progress, improvement, and future are anything but. Katherine Onorato (1999, Bay Area) came to one of the city's worst-performing schools and witnessed a major turnaround in her four years of teaching. The additions of a full-time social worker, a conflict manager, a technology team, and new teacher support staff began the process of creating problem-solving teams. As resources increased, more teachers have stayed from year to year. In classrooms that were previously revolving doors with teachers in and out, teachers were retained. More stability translated to a more supportive school climate. Suspension rates decreased dramatically. Katherine concluded, "It's like night and day, looking at my first year and my third year."

Teach For America has taught me the importance of optimism. As a teacher, you have to believe that change is possible and then commit yourself to bringing about that change.

—Wendy Eberhart (2000, North Carolina)

Corps members, like Mike Wang (1999, Southern Louisiana), reflect on their hope for the future as they watch the radical improvement of districts and states over time. After two years of teaching in Baton Rouge, Mike began working as the education policy advisor to Louisiana Governor Mike Foster. He makes recommendations on education policy directly to the governor and serves as the governor's liaison to the state legislature, teachers' unions, and other groups.

When Mike began teaching, it was common to read front-page newspaper articles that cast a negative light on education. Since then, Mike has noticed that the "negative attitude still exists, but it is countered by the positives more and more." Mike has witnessed Louisiana at the incipient stages of wide-reaching broad educational reform. As a teacher, Mike was a critic of Louisiana's recent shift to high-stakes testing, but he has undergone "a dramatic turnaround from the way I felt about some educational policies as a classroom teacher to how I feel now." Mike now points to high-stakes testing with vociferous support; "It's fundamentally sound policy. Unfortunately in some troubled districts, it's a case of sound policy being poorly implemented." Under Governor Foster, Louisiana has committed nearly $40 million in new funding to serve almost 10,000 new pre–K students in an effort to expand high-quality early childhood education. According to the National Education Association, over one-third more third graders are reading at or above grade level in 2002 than in 1998. There have been tremendous strides in teacher pay, with increases of over $9,500 since 1996. Louisiana was cited by *Princeton Review* as ranking seventh in the nation in test and standards alignment; by *Education Week* as ranking fifth in the nation in accountability; twelfth in improving teacher quality; and as receiving an "A" for accountability from the Fordham Foundation. Nine out of ten schools showed improvement in the most recent school improvement cycle, and on the most recent National Assessment of Education Progress, Louisiana fourth graders were most improved in the nation on math and eighth graders were among students from only five states in the country to improve in both reading and math. Louisiana has progressed at a faster pace than virtually any other state in the union.

For Mike, hope is very much alive:

> The most important thing that I took away from my Teach For America experience, the thing that drives what I do every day is that this is not a futile effort. Despite the challenges and obstacles, educational reform can work and progress is possible.

chapter eleven

one day: the road ahead for teach for america

Teach For America is impacting our nation's students in positive ways. Corps members see the value of communities like the ones in which we teach. Corps members realize we all have the responsibility to grow and learn together, and that as Americans we all are tied to each other through the network of communities. These children, in poor areas, are our future just as much as the children from our neighborhoods back home.

—Anne Sung (2000, Rio Grande Valley)

At its 1990 inception, Teach For America was a revolutionary organization. Never before had young college graduates with no background in teaching or education been seen as a viable resource to address the nation's glaring educational inequity. Additionally, its grassroots creation made Teach For America innovative. Recent college graduates worked from scratch to translate their visions and ideals into reality. They pounded on the doors of politicians and executives whose financial support could bring their ideas to life. And they were convinced that educational inequity was a matter of social justice; in a 2003 interview, president and founder Wendy Kopp stated, "Educational equity must become this generation's civil rights issue."

Teach For America may be losing some of its revolutionary identity. It is no longer a new kid on the block in debates over public education. It has grown increasingly corporate, drawing up five-year plans and strictly monitoring its budget. With huge media attention comes enormous fund-raising ability. In 2002, Teach For America raised $21 million in annual funding. Teach For America gains the attention of top politicians, celebrities, and donors. Its Board of Directors is a virtual who's who list of CEOs of major corporations, chairpersons of influential businesses, and noteworthy philanthropists. As the organization grows older, its power and recognition escalates.

Even though their grassroots have been outgrown, Teach For America remains at the forefront of education because of its leadership in alternative education. Its innovation rests in the ability to attract top quality candidates who may otherwise not have considered teaching. Its success lies in making teaching an attractive choice, even if it is only for two years. And last, Teach For America has tapped into a legitimate pool of teaching candidates in its alternative pathway into the classroom.

attracting quality students

Teach For America's accomplishment comes from the cadre of people who care about education and remain somehow connected to the movement.
—Seth Kugel (1992, Los Angeles)

Without Teach For America, corps members like Dakota Prosch, Morty Ballen, and Tracy Brisson may never have found their way into classrooms where they were desperately needed. What corps members lack in formal training and in pedagogical theory they make up for in compassion, motivation, and energy.

Dakota Prosch (2000, Chicago) always wanted to be a teacher. She came to Teach For America thinking it was "the best way to start teaching right away." She was one of the few corps members to work in two different schools during her commitment. All of the components existed to impede student learning, including teacher turnover, massive overcrowding, and poor leadership. Her sixth grade students had been taught by a long-term substitute the previous year. "They were so used to people leaving them that they thought I'd be next in line." Half of her students had failed a previous grade. To alleviate crowding, the school ran on a year-round schedule, where every three months one track of classes took a month off while their classroom was occupied by another track of students. As a result, some teachers moved to new classrooms every month. Dakota wasn't hired until the third month of the first trimester. Additionally, her principal was unsupportive and borderline antagonistic. "My principal resented that I came to teaching through Teach For America. Every successful thing that I did became a thorn in his side. If I had failed as a teacher, he would have been satisfied."

Dakota remembered her first month as being "miserable."

> My kids ate me alive. They wouldn't sit down. They were yelling and throwing things. Before Christmas break, I asked them to write me a paragraph telling me why I should return after the vacation. They all wrote the paragraph, and when I came back things were better. The kids were ultimately on my side.

Dakota set the audacious goal that all of her students would pass sixth grade. She reassessed her teaching style, taught her students the importance of hard work, and did whatever it took to push her class forward:

> I scrapped the old irrelevant reading books we had and brought in articles that met my students at their reading level and interests. We read articles about rock stars and teenage issues. I focused math lessons on realistic projects, like buying and selling and the stock market. Every day I made allusions to how hard we were working. That work ethic brought us together. I kept them on track with incentives—tickets to win prizes and good citizenship rewards.

Dakota met her students at school an hour early for extra math help and stayed an hour late for reading tutorials. "Some kids were receiving seven extra hours of school a week. That's the only way to do it." The diligence of the students and their teacher reaped rewards; all of her students passed the Iowa Test of Basic Skills, a test used to benchmark student levels.

Dakota's Teach For America experience confirmed her desire to be a lifelong teacher. An advocate for the professionalism of teaching, Dakota returned to school to pursue her master's in teaching and continues to teach in a Chicago charter school.

In Baton Rouge, Morty Ballen (1992, Southern Louisiana) saw schools that weren't working and leaders who weren't taking responsibility. Negative school environments and teachers who didn't expect the absolute best from students propelled his anger. Yet despite these factors, Morty watched students overcome obstacles and concluded that, "the challenges to being poor are not stopping kids from achieving at high levels." Fueled by his fervor to start a new school, he earned a master's in education at Columbia University's Teachers College. In 1999, he left teaching to lay the foundations for his vision of a new charter school in Manhattan's Lower East Side. His philosophy was to "give kids a shot at the American dream, that good education is a right, not a privilege."

EXPLORE Charter School opened in August 2002 with 168 students in grades K through 3. Morty continues to address at-risk students; 80% of the students are eligible for free or reduced meals. In the school where EXPLORE recruited from, 76% of students are not reading at grade level and 70% do not meet the math standards. Morty's belief that "teaching a child to read is inspiring and exciting" is the foundation for strong early literacy strategies. EXPLORE Charter School aims to provide students with the skills and knowledge they need to enter a high school of their choice.

Morty pointed to Teach For America for stimulating his sense of responsibility:

From Teach For America I could see with perseverance and hard work, anything can happen—schools can be built literally from scratch. I guess Teach For America provides me with ongoing proof of a sense of possibility of a better tomorrow and that it is up to me to get to work to ensure that that better tomorrow actually happens. I learned that, as a citizen of a country that makes a promise that all children have the right to life, liberty, and the pursuit of happiness, then, as a citizen, it is my responsibility to do what I can to breathe life into this promise—to make it come alive. I also learned from Teach for America that one person really can move forward and upward through hard work and determination.

And even those corps members who leave the classroom become advocates for public education wherever they go. Tracy Brisson (1997, New York) came to Washington Heights aspiring to "be the best teacher I could be." When fellow corps members scattered to find housing throughout Manhattan, Tracy decided to live within the community where she taught, only blocks away from school, reasoning, "living in the community gave me a better understanding of my students and their families." In her first year of teaching, New York City schools passed new performance-based standards. One standard held fourth graders to reading and comprehending twenty-five books. Some teachers created checklists to count books, but for Tracy, "it was important to me that they really understood every book they read." It wasn't enough for her students to memorize multiplication tables. They needed to understand why they were learning them—the logic behind their knowledge. On Saturdays, she took students to local bookstores to attend author readings. She made home visits, chaperoned birthday parties, and rewarded well-behaved students with lunch trips to McDonalds'. In the first week of summer vacation of her second year, she took her students to areas of Manhattan where they had never been and were eager to explore—Chinatown, SoHo, Washington Square, and Little Italy. For Tracy, "the job never stopped."

Tracy is now in her sixth year of working for the New York City Public School System. After teaching for two years, she worked for one year in the Budget Office of the New York City School System. She is now in her third year as a program manager for the Office of Alternative Certification, which manages the largest alternative certification program in the country, the New York City Teaching Fellows. With a master's in public administration and finance, Tracy feels "like I can't leave public education until things are better."

It is with this force of leaders that Teach For America gives young people a real world understanding of the realities of education and then holds them to pursue change. Laura Perkins (1999, Bay Area) explains, "After two years, Teach For America creates a group of people who have a profound understanding of issues of inequity, adequacy, and social justice. They create a force of well-educated people who think, "'I was there. How do we make things better?'"

The power of Teach For America is in its ideas and ideals. The genius is in its leadership. The strength is in its membership, the folks that do this work and carry out the mission.

—Jason Levy (1993, Houston)

teaching as a community profession

Teach For America gave me a tremendous amount of respect for teachers and for their ongoing work.

—Rowell Levy (1998, Phoenix)

Equally powerful is Teach For America's ability to make teaching a viable and competitive profession for top college grads. Teach For America has gotten a generation of people to seriously consider teaching as a means to promote social equality. Rob Reich (1992, Houston) sees this played out at Stanford University, where he is an assistant professor in political science. His involvement with Teach For America comes from his willingness to speak to his undergraduate students about his experience. As a result, he has witnessed dozens of his students apply to and join Teach For America. "In colleges now, undergrads are looking to teaching, and Teach For America, as the latest civil rights movement of their generation."

Teach For America makes teaching a competitive profession to people who wouldn't otherwise have seen teaching in low-income areas as an attractive career option.

—Melea Bollman (1998, Rio Grande Valley)

a new pool of teachers

Teach For America is experimenting. They're trying to make a real effort and turn teacher education on its head. TFA is almost a standing criticism of education schools. I dare anyone to point to a program that truly trains people well for urban and poor rural schools. I am right there with the critics when they ask about the problems with Teach For America. But I ask them to turn that same critical light on themselves and ask, "Are your graduates making as many strides towards student achievements as Teach For America is?" I wish education schools would spend as much time assessing themselves as they do TFA. If one day education schools are able to put Teach For America out of business, I'd say Amen. That's a day we all need.

—Tom Shepley (1992, Baltimore)

Just as Teach For America has made teaching a more attractive profession, it has also gained credibility as an alternative route into teaching. This theory was supported in August 2001, when a research group based at the Hoover Institute of Stanford University released a study which called Teach For America "a viable and valuable source of teachers." The study examined TFA teachers in Houston and determined that they performed as well as, and in many cases, better than non-TFA teachers. Using test scores for quantitative data, the analysis studied whether the average TFA teacher affected students' test scores differently than the average non-TFA teacher. Dr. Macke Raymond of the Stanford's Hoover Institute explained the conclusion that on average, the impact of having a TFA teacher was always positive:

> There is a strong body of evidence that new teachers take a few years before creating academic gains for their students. One critique of Teach For America is that corps members walk into the class deaf, dumb, and blind. If this were so, we'd see an adverse effect on students. Yes, Teach For America teachers are new to the classroom, but so are others in these placements. We decided to see what we would find out by putting TFA teachers head to head versus other new teachers—certified or not. We found that uncredentialed teachers, specifically those in the Teach For America subset, made significant statistical increases for their students at the elementary level, though the results were not as strong at the middle school level.

Raymond pointed to several areas where the results of her work play out:

> With these results, we can conclude that we have a large pool of talented and motivated people who haven't gone through traditional teacher programs, but are likely to be positive sources for classrooms that need teachers. A lot of districts could make Teach For America an option if they are convinced of the quality of its candidates. Moreover, Teach For America has a phenomenal galvanizing effect on traditional schools of education. We can see these results as a way to prompt traditional schools of education to increase the quality of their product.

In 2002 the Department of Education granted Teach For America a $4.75 million grant to fund expansion efforts. With the tremendous need for teachers, Teach For America is one piece to increase the human capital that comes into public education. Corps members like Rowell Levy (1998, Phoenix) see Teach For America as a positive factor:

> Teach For America is not the one solution. It's one of many solutions. It's the proof that we need to try a lot of things to better educate our nation's children. To bring about true educational reform, we need a lot of irons in the fire.

Teach For America is right in thinking that there are alternative ways to train teachers.
                        —Hillary Roselund (1999, Washington, D.C.)

how do they do it?

Teach For America relies on youth, idealism, and enthusiasm to compensate for experience. And that theory works to a certain extent. With TFA, it's trial by fire. It takes a certain personality to make it in Teach For America. It's a sink or swim mentality.
                        —Aaron Amitin (2001, New York)

In only thirteen years, Teach For America has gone from a floundering organization with constant funding worries to a powerhouse hailed by presidents and political leaders. Teach For America has revealed that success comes from constant reflection and self-assessment, from a pressing sense of urgency about the mission, and from listening to voices from within and from outside of the corps. Scott Joftus (1990, New York) explained, "Teach For America has taken a lot of hits. It has worked to resolve and acknowledge these issues rather than be hyper-

defensive. Its responsiveness and its constant reflection is the top reason for its success."

*TFA has shown that it can roll up its sleeves to think intelligently with
a good critical eye to think about things that will make schools better.*
                                   —Chris Barbic (1992, Rio Grande Valley)

Adhering to adaptability, Teach For America has made significant
strides in corps member preparation and accountability. Amy Wilson
(1992, Baltimore) provided a sense of Teach For America's reflection
and evolution. Amy is a rare voice not only in her transition from a
corps member to a teacher trainer who now oversees incoming corps
members, but also because of her long-term stay of ten years in her
original region. She explained:

> The incoming corps has better concrete skills. Early on, corps members
> came in with idealistic, nebulous goals. Teach For America lately has
> been driven by the larger forces of education including accountability.
> Unless we get specific, there's no measurability. We are constantly ask-
> ing how to show that what we are doing makes a difference in student
> achievement. Corps members go in every day thinking, "What will I do
> today to get my kids to learn?" We see it all through the lens of "What
> am I teaching? What are my students learning?"

*Every year, Teach For America improves its training. Every year, corps
members are better prepared. Every year, the support systems and structures get better.*
                                   —Anne Sung (2000, Rio Grande Valley)

The improvement in training over time is apparent to Jason Levy
(1993, Houston), who compares his training with that of the corps
members that he now oversees as an assistant principal:

Corps members today are much better prepared than I was. The training is much more substantial. Corps members have more resources to draw on and the pool of candidates is more diverse. Folks come to the organization more familiar with education in general and with a more realistic understanding of tools, skills, and theories.

Teach For America quickly corrected its early mistakes and improved the entire range of support that corps members now receive. As noted by Leigh Anne Fraley (1992, Southern Louisiana) in her two years working in the Washington, D.C., regional office, "Things have really changed and gotten better." Regional offices have strengthened to give corps members more accessibility to Program Directors. Classroom visits are more frequent, as are check-in phone calls. Corps members go through Induction, a regional orientation in which they are acquainted with their districts and their communities. Monthly All Corps Meetings provide professional development workshops, available resources, and upcoming events of interest. Corps members share ideas and reflect on best practice strategies in learning teams, organized by grade level and subject area. Mentor teachers serve as sounding boards and voices of experience. Monthly newsletters connect corps members with teachers to observe and provide information on available resources and grants. A wide range of social events connect corps members on personal levels. University partnerships have solidified, allowing corps members to work toward certification and master's degrees during their commitments.

Moreover, Teach For America continues to think critically about the issues that corps members face, exemplified by the Diversity Task Force. Spearheaded by Nicole Baker (1991, Los Angeles), the Diversity Task Force critically examines Teach For America's dialogues about race, culture, and ethnicity. In 1991, Nicole sensed that "Teach For America was not an organization that truly welcomed me, as an African-American woman, or valued my experiences. As a result, I became fairly disconnected from the organization and my fellow alumni for the next several years." In 1999, she worked to form the Diversity Task Force to address the diversity topics that affect the communities that Teach For America reaches. The priorities became issues of race and class, because they were most relevant to the organization's mission. The Diversity Task Force defined diversity as the full range of identities and backgrounds, including race and ethnicity, class, sexual orientation, gender, age, religion, political opinion, language, and issues of disabilities. They next mapped out how race and class issues pertained to every step of the Teach For America experience, from recruitment and selection to training and classroom commitment. Three overarching priorities emerged: 1) to increase the extent to which its corps members and staff are sensitive to the diversity in classrooms and communities, 2) to increase the ethnic and racial diversity of corps members, staff, and board members, and 3) to ensure that all individuals are welcomed, valued, and engaged.

In 2002, Teach For America created the Special Education Task Force, which was born out of the conviction that most, if not all, corps members will work with students with exceptionalities and that the strategies that special education teachers used were applicable to all classrooms and all learners. Liz Marcell (1999, Rio Grande Valley), Melissa Dyckes Storm (1994, Southern Louisiana), and Michelle Koyama (1997, Rio Grande Valley) hammered out a proposal. The result was a six-person task force, made up of special educators with a variety of teaching experiences. The Task Force accessed alums and regional directors to distribute a list of phenomenal special educators with varied areas of expertise who could answer corps members' questions about students with exceptionalities.

The support does not stop after the two years, but rather Teach For America has strengthened its alumni network to connect alumni and current corps members to the larger mission. In 1997, Teach For America hired Tim Gamory (1995, New York) to define and build the network. Tim envisioned a network of people with shared experiences who could "work together to figure out what levers to pull to affect systemic change." When he began, the contact information and whereabouts were known for only 20% of alumni. Over the next four years, Tim created a strong infrastructure based on an up-to-date alumni directory, an alumni newsletter, a website, and regional alumni chapters. In 2002, Teach For America created the office of Career and Civic Opportunities to encourage alumni to take meaningful career opportunities that promote long-term change.

the road ahead

With thirteen years of growth and evolution under its belt, Teach For America is at a crucial crossroads. Teach For America believes its foundation is solid enough to look ahead to the future and reach more students in more low-income areas. The road ahead brings corps expansion both in size and in regions. By 2005, two thousand corps members will teach in over twenty-three regions nationwide. With this increase, the corps will number over 3,800 members a year.

At its tenth anniversary summit meeting, Teach For America alumni, corps members, and staff gathered to reflect on the lessons learned in the first ten years and their application to the future. Wendy Kopp, president and founder of Teach For America, reflected on the steep learning curve Teach For America climbed in its first ten years as well as the road ahead:

> In our tenth year, we finally could begin to look ahead on where next to go. We were receiving offers from funders who told us, "If you grow to scale, we will increase our funding." We realized that through growing, we could acquire not only more financial resources, but more human resources as well. We were operating on a deep belief that Teach For America, in its current form, had a powerful short-term and long-term impact, and to increase that impact, we would have to increase its scale by placing the strongest critical mass in the highest-need areas. Yet to be a truly effective movement, we need to create dramatic gains for students in low-income areas in order to close the achievement gap. Teach For America is building the movement to eliminate educational inequality. As long as the achievement gap exists in this country, we need more teachers who are willing to go above and beyond the call of duty to propel their students forward.

Allie Rogovin (1995, Houston) of Teach For America's National Recruitment Team, explained that Teach For America's expansion is due to the continued presence of educational inequity:

> It really boils down to the fact that our country is basically in the same state we were when Teach For America was founded thirteen years ago. The educational gap between low-income and high-income students is just as wide. Over time, our corps members and alumni have been enormously successful, working from within education and from other fields to provide more opportunities to children growing up in low-income areas. Given the fact that the gap is still as wide and the fact that our corps members and alumni have been successful, Teach For America feels a tremendous sense of urgency to do more. We need to place more corps members in more locations. Initially, our biggest concern with expansion was whether or not we could attract enough highly qualified candidates. In 2002, with applications numbering 14,000, we got the boost of confidence we needed.

Like so much of Teach For America, the plans for expansion are hotly debated by corps members themselves. Critics, like Sarah Fang (1996, Phoenix) state, "TFA shouldn't be funneling more uncredentialed teachers into the classroom. It should be working to end itself out of existence." Clare Pinchin (1999, Bay Area) confessed her hesitation stems from the lack of training and experience:

> The expansion idea is scary to me. My experience made me realize that teachers need tons of experience before coming to the classroom. I'm not saying that people can't be successful without this experience, but it takes its toll and becomes so challenging and emotionally upsetting. Expansion without thought and a connection to the realities of what is going on in classrooms nationwide is a problem. Small things can be controlled, but if we grow too big then people can't stay on top of the details.

Other factors are the quality of candidates and the need for support. Tia Lendo (2000, North Carolina) identifies herself as on the camp of growing, but not growing too fast; "I hope that expansion will not mean that quality of candidates goes down, in an effort to merely push numbers." Dakota Prosch (2000, Chicago) explained:

> I hope expansion doesn't mean that Teach For America will be less intimate and personal. I have witnessed the Chicago corps grow over three years from thirty corps members to two hundred. With more people, more people may fall through the cracks and not get the support they need. It's a trade-off though, because expansion also means that more people are in classrooms being successful.

Susannah Nichols (2002, Detroit) believed that Teach For America's vision is genuine, though "expansion is ridiculous." Her opinion comes from her own experience in Detroit's 2002 charter corps, where corps members were not placed until after the start of the school year, where corps members are considered by the district not as regular teachers but rather Extended Substitutes in Regular Positions, and where corps members have little job security and lower pay. She acknowledged the difficulty of the situation of being in the charter corps:

> As TFA corps members, you do sign up for challenges and inconveniences and some instances are completely understandable. Teach For America brought us out to Detroit without having truly assessed the needs of the district. What was particularly troubling is that we were consistently given one set of information, only to have those conditions changed at the last minute. Teach For America is so consumed with the idea of expanding that they are doing it without responsibility. I think TFA believes that expanding rapidly will increase their impact, but the lack of preparedness with which they enter some sites makes it difficult for their mission to be achieved.

Many corps members support expansion only with stipulations. Amy Christie (2001, New York) advocates for expansion only if Teach For America carefully evaluates the impact on students and the continued training and support for corps members:

> As Teach For America looks ahead towards expansion, they need to think about whether this expansion will benefit the students. Are our students improving as the organization grows? The focus of the organization needs to be the best possible ways to support the current corps so they can be the best possible teachers. Teach For America is moving in the right direction, but I think they're still in the baby stages of evaluating what is best regarding the training of their teachers.

Sarah Van Orman (1990, Rural Georgia) warns Teach For America to proceed with caution. She questions people who join Teach For America as a stepping stone into other careers, though she readily admitted she was one of those people:

> It doesn't help for Teach For America to go into schools on a sort of Peace Corps mission. It may help individual corps members, but not schools themselves. But the idea of Teach For America should be to train people to stay in education. Teach For America is never going to fix public schools, but it should be a vocal advocate for what is going on in schools. If there is a continued focus on training to support corps members to stay in the classroom, I support the expansion plans.

But the inarguable fact remains: Our country needs teachers. *Education Week* estimates that by 2011, more than two million new teachers will be needed. Supporters of the expansion return to this logic as the go-ahead for Teach For America's growth. As explained by Autumn De Vos (1997, Baltimore), "so many schools and kids need dedicated, innovative, energetic teachers who believe in them." Anina Robb (1996, New York) pointed out the following:

The good that corps members can do in two years in the classroom by far outbalances the major criticism often directed at them, namely that most only stay for two years. I understand and acknowledge how turnover induced by TFA can be a problem. However, there are other things that young idealistic people can show children besides content area knowledge that are important aspects of educating our students. The sad reality is that other people aren't jumping in to fill these positions. Furthermore, the positives that a Teach For America teacher brings to an under-resourced school by far outweigh the negatives. If there are young people to take on these challenging teaching positions, that's fabulous. We should harness and use their energy.

Art Schuhart (1990, New York) argued that expansion is a matter of supply and demand.

The reality is that we will need two million teachers in the next ten years and we better grab them from wherever we can find them. Think of Teach For America as the National Guard of education, a supplemental source of teachers. Teach For America is definitely a productive program that is well worth saving. It brings imaginative, motivated young teachers into the classroom, which isn't always being done in schools of higher education.

And those corps members who support expansion keep in mind what such expansion means in the larger context of public education: the sad reality that we cannot attract and keep certified teachers. Lauren Kaler (1995, Phoenix) explained, "I hope there will be a day with no need for Teach For America, a day when quality people will be attracted to teaching with higher salaries and equal resources."

the factors to consider

In education today, there is a trend toward sophistication in accountability and measurability. Teach For America is going with that flow. They are better equipped now to be smart about their training practices. They have also improved their ability to access the resources that are available to teachers and their ability to connect their teachers with these resources.

—Melea Bollman (1998, Rio Grande Valley)

Just as the road ahead brings expansion, it also brings the need to address larger systemic factors regarding educational issues. At first Teach For America may have been about simply filling teaching vacancies, however, it has refined its role to narrow the achievement gap. Mark Williams (2000, New Jersey), in his role as the Program Director for the 2002 New Jersey corps, testified to the trend of achievement:

> Teach For America has much more of an orientation towards achievement and significant gains. I didn't notice it so much in my own corps year of 2000, but as a Corps Member Adviser in 2002 and as a part of the regional staff, the talk of significant gains is all over the place. It's a part of the language. We are pushing people to think about what they are doing in their classrooms and how that translates to student achievement. It's not enough to have twenty happy students in your classroom. The question becomes, What are you accomplishing with those twenty students? We must send the message to corps members that it's okay to face challenges along the way, but we must push the mentality of moving children forward.

In addition, Teach For America must continue to grapple with other sensitive issues, primarily the disconnect between corps members and communities and the turnover that may result from two-year commitments. First, some corps members point to a philosophical problem in

Teach For America's basic premise, and question whether it continues to foster elitist propositions. Andrew Greenhill (1991, Houston) pointed to the disconnection in the idea "that the best and brightest can somehow have a better ability to teach inner-city kids." He believes the nature of the problem is that too often corps members have no real connection to their students:

> I can't help but wonder about the logic behind sending a college grad from an Iowa cornfield with a degree in computer science to Watts to teach fifth grade math. I hope Teach For America puts forth a concerted effort to find people with similar backgrounds to the populations we teach as opposed to combing through elite universities to find applicants.

Alex Caputo-Pearl (1990, Los Angeles) disapproved of the elitist feel that Teach For America conveys:

> TFA still has a best and brightest feel to it. It sets things up as the greatest people—college educated, the majority being white—going out to save the world. I remain critical of how Teach For America plays to the good side of service orientation, but it's too paternalistic—it seems to send the message that, "Isn't it too bad that poor people can't get their schools together?"

Teach For America confirmed Alex's desire to do "progressive, antiracist political work." As a teacher in the Los Angeles Unified School District, Alex spearheads the Coalition for Educational Justice as a way to merge teaching and politics. He encourages Teach For America to "lose its politically cautious stance. There are ways TFA could creatively open spaces for political dialogue and allow for explicit critiques of government and political structures."

Dennis Guikema (1994, Bay Area) found faults in the basic premise of Teach For America, "the philosophy that it holds the answers, that community problems are solvable by people from outside the community." He hopes to see a day when recruitment comes from within the communities that Teach For America serves, rather than drawing disproportionately from white and upper-class candidates:

> I'm not saying that there's no place for a wealthy white person in urban education, but perhaps Teach For America should use its incredible media exposure and economic resources to recruit from within the communities where we place. They could work to build satellite programs to pool state and junior college students to move on to teaching. The retention rate of teachers in low-income areas would be higher that way and the immediate impact would be greater because there wouldn't be the cultural divide corps members face now. When it's all said and done, Teach For America needs to ask itself what will the communities get out of two-year stints?

Perhaps Teach For America's most troublesome dilemma pertains to two-year commitments, which corps members, principals, and critics often point to as increasing turnover. Principal Paul Johnson identified himself as a proponent of Teach For America expansion and looks to have more corps members placed at his school. However, his remaining concern is the brevity of the two-year commitment:

> One thing that I'd like to see Teach For America address is to do more to encourage corps members to stay more than two years. Teaching is a profession that requires five years to learn. Two years is not enough time. Moreover, our kids need continuity and consistency, which doesn't come in the turnover of two years.

Aaron Amitin (2001, New York) sees Teach For America's biggest downside as the two-year minimum, which is an "inhibitor of consistent learning for students."

> Teach For America promotes inconsistency. The quality is good, but the length isn't. I think people do Teach For America because it's an experience, not because they want to be a career teacher.

David Wakelyn (1990, Los Angeles) explained:

> Yes, our schools will need a million new people, but not a million peo-
> ple who come and go and come and go. Cycling bodies in and out of
> the same positions every two years is not a solution to the problem of
> the "leaky bucket." It's at best, a less than adequate plug.

> *The solution to public education is building up stronger schools, not*
> *building up a bigger corps of people who may leave after two years.*
> —Jeff Max (1999, New Orleans)

But perhaps the problem of retention has very little to do with Teach
For America and much more to do with the realities of public education. A recent survey in *Education Week* revealed that 20% of new
teachers leave the classroom after three years, and 50% quit after five.
Perhaps these young teachers have seen too much in urban and rural
classrooms to know that teaching is just too difficult to be a lifelong
career.

the outlook

Teach For America is a valuable contribution to the ongoing debate of
how to fix our nation's schools, yet it is a progress in a movement that
has a long way to go. Teach For America raises more questions than it
answers, questions about the achievement gap, the critical need for
teachers, and how to recruit quality teachers. It reveals both the realities of public education and the possibilities for the future. The mere
presence of Teach For America indicates the gravity of our nation's educational crisis; if urban and rural schools were able to find enough
qualified teachers, Teach For America wouldn't exist. Yet as Teach For
America corps members continue to make significant academic gains
with their students and as alumni take on leadership positions to promote long-term change, they are the proof that passion to serve is the
first step in combating educational inequity. Teach For America is our

constant reminder that the work in public education is far from done and that a sense of urgency is a crucial component in ensuring that one day, all children in this nation will have the opportunity to attain an excellent education.

afterword

This process has been about me being a student to my students and to my fellow faculty.

—Mike Fisher (1999, Rio Grande Valley)

Like many Teach For America corps members, I continue to look back at my experience in a variety of lights. I remember it, reflect upon it, and sometimes struggle with it. I have yet to find a way to summarize the depth of the experience, so instead I ask myself the really hard questions. How much of a difference did I make on my students? Did I gain more from the experience of learning from them than they did from having me as their teacher? One thing is certain: I am incredibly thankful that I made the commitment. In the most profound way, Teach For America gave my life a meaningful direction. It transformed me from a young college graduate, enveloped in self-satisfaction, to an individual fueled by social activism. My classroom experience was the hardest two years of my life, full of intellectual, social, emotional, and professional challenges. In the blink of an eye, I was sent to Oakland, California, where, just as Ray Owens (1991, Los Angeles) predicted in his 1991 summer institute speech, my college credentials and my background didn't matter to my students, my fellow teachers, or community leaders. In all of my idealism and romanticism upon joining Teach For America, I had overlooked the most important lesson that I would learn: Teaching is hard work.

My first year of teaching was a disappointment and an uphill battle. I barely knew how to teach Abby about long vowels, how to help Armando with a profound learning disability, or how to convince Cynthia not to join a neighborhood gang. I worked as hard as I possibly could, but still I felt like Mike Fisher (1999, Rio Grande Valley) whose candid self-doubt seemed taboo with Teach For America:

> I'm ashamed of my first year of teaching. I didn't dive into the experience as much as I could have. And I'll admit that I thought of quitting my first year. I had a lot of emotional and social struggles in that first year.

And though my second year was vastly better, I still felt like something was missing. I still cannot point to significant gains that my students made on standardized tests. I did not take my students on a field trip to Europe, or secure a substantial grant to bring computers to classrooms, or lead my students to victory in the district basketball championship. I was frustrated that the end results didn't seem to match up to my effort, as explained by Molly Blank (1998, Washington, D.C.):

> I can say that I was a good teacher. I gave it my blood, sweat, and tears. My students didn't do well on standardized tests and it devastated me. I taught my kids, but I didn't make the achievement gap narrow.

As a rookie teacher struggling to survive, I internalized a message that seemed to trickle down from above: In Teach For America, there was no room for failure. I felt like I was not living up to its standards of high expectations and significant gains. Even more disappointingly, I felt that my students deserved so much more out of a teacher. I felt like Justin Arnold (2002, New York), who stated, "It was like I was in a bicycle race against Lance Armstrong, going up this huge hill. I jumped on this bike not knowing how to work it and I was told to go." That feeling led me to stray from the organization in my first year of teaching. I recall going to corps meetings where I was inundated with the success stories of those around me, and thinking, "I'll never live up to those standards." And though I knew Teach For America corps members were sharing their success stories to inspire, I felt the other extreme—intimidation. It was only later that I discovered that I wasn't alone in my feelings. Amy Wilson (1992, Baltimore) stated, "I am frustrated by the attention that Teach For America, as an organization, gives to its superstars. They absolutely should highlight their incredible successes, yet that can be alienating to someone who is plugging away day to day." Allison Serafin (2001, Houston) illuminated the risk in high expectations:

> There is so much pressure on the incoming corps. TFA teachers have a huge burden, these expectations where simply going into the classroom and doing their best simply isn't enough. They have to go above and beyond for their students. It's bothersome and a difficult pill to swallow, when you hear these amazing stories of what people have done and you think, How will I get there? Will I get there? You have to realize that you can't compare yourself to others in that regard.

However, just as I recall the moments of struggle, I recall the moments of clarity, understanding, and newly acquired wisdom. One memory sticks with me still, when I learned an invaluable lesson about the grace and resilience of my students. The following is one of my favorite stories to come out of my first year of teaching.

On a rainy December morning, I found myself staring at the clock anxiously waiting for the lunch bell to ring. Instead of my usual morning schedule, I was spending fourth period in the school's auditorium. My sixth grade students were rehearsing for the upcoming Winter Concert, and the music teacher had requested my presence for crowd control and supervision. I had spent the last half-hour telling my students to stop talking, to follow directions, and to keep their hands to themselves. I was frustrated and couldn't wait for lunch, when I could nurse my throbbing headache. My students were lined up along the makeshift risers and I sat below, in the first row of seats, watching them on stage. The rundown auditorium was drafty; blasts of wind blew in from broken windows. My students were supposed to be watching the music teacher for instructions, but really their attention was everywhere else. Jacqueline and Jessie whispered to each other, Rene poked Tony in the back, and Eduardo gazed off dreamily into the distance. Quickly losing my patience, I instructed my students to pay attention.

Suddenly the piano sounded out three booming chords, the music teacher raised her hands, and my students began to sing. For one brief moment, they stopped their fidgeting and horseplay, and lifted their voices to sing. My eighty-three sixth grade students formed one off-key, out-of-tune chorus. I listened to them sing Louis Armstrong's classic, "What a Wonderful World." Their singing was terrible. They rushed through the song and were two beats ahead of the pianist, who kept having to play catch-up. The low notes were flat and the high notes were piercingly shrill, but there was something soothing in their music. When they sang the last note, I clapped loudly for them, my applause echoing in the empty auditorium. Most gave me a strange look, but a few of them smiled back.

The loud sounding of the lunch bell interrupted my applause. My students jumped off the risers and sprinted for the door, not heeding my commands of "Walk" or "Slow down." In eight seconds, the auditorium was empty and I headed back to my classroom. A few moments later, when I sat at my desk eating my sandwich and grading papers, there was a soft knock at the door. I glanced up and saw eleven-year-old Tina poking her head in the door.

"Ms. Ness, I left my backpack here," she mumbled quietly. Tina, a Chinese student who spoke very little English, was very shy.

"Come on in and grab it," I replied.

Tina walked to her desk and gathered her belongings while I continued with my work. I scarcely paid attention to her as she headed back out of the room. One hand on the doorknob, she called my name again. I answered her call, but did not even bother to look up.

"Ms. Ness, I want it to be a wonderful world," she said.

"Yeah, Tina, that's a nice song that you guys are singing," I answered.

"No, Ms. Ness. It's not just a song. I want this to be a wonderful world." With that, Tina walked out the door.

That one moment truly changed my perspective. For so many of my sixth grade students, it was not a wonderful world. They spent their childhoods surrounded by violence, gangs, racial tension, and poverty in a drug-ridden neighborhood of Oakland. They watched alcoholic fathers abuse their mothers. They shared a ramshackle two-bedroom apartment with their grandparents, three aunts, one uncle, and four siblings. They came to the United States in the bed of a pickup truck, illegal Mexican immigrants following crop harvests. Instead of childhood innocence, these students witnessed the realities of an unequal world. But they were never bogged down in such sadness. Instead they demonstrated courage and perseverance to overcome obstacles. Juan returned to school every day, after losing his baby brother in a house fire. Alan participated in class discussions while battling the post-traumatic stress of growing up in war-torn Bosnia. Mindy read *Harry Potter* all by herself. They never gave up the hope that, one day, it would be a wonderful world.

I left the classroom after two years. It was time to go. I came to Oakland with a delicate balance between outrage and optimism. I was outraged by the injustice I saw, the poor conditions, the inequity based purely on race and class. Yet I still clung to my optimism, my hope in the progress that was already being made and the awareness that my students were making huge strides in the face of adversity. However, in the middle of my second year, I lost my outrage. In a sort of coping mechanism, I learned to shrug off too much. I was less outraged that my special education students were not receiving the intervention they deserved and needed. I was less bothered by the politics, the daily frustrations, the paperwork. And I was not comfortable with the changes I saw in myself. While there is a risk of carrying too much outrage, there was a purpose for my outrage; I used it to push myself harder and to promote desparately needed change. I was scared that any more time in the classroom would leave me dismissive, ineffective, and complacent. Teach For America made me realize that I wanted to devote the rest of my life to the pursuit of social justice, but that if I didn't take a break from it to regain my strength and conviction, I might not return.

In leaving the classroom, I came to understand that my commitment to Teach For America was not over. When I applied as a college senior, I assuaged my self-doubt with a simple statement. "It's only two years." I was wrong. Teach For America forever changed the person I would be. Though I had always had an interest in social justice, Teach For America steered me toward an important path. It became my point of reference. Those two years have turned into a long-term fascination with public education and the work that Teach For America is doing. The two years of Teach For America were a beginning, not an ending.

I still look at the organization not only with intrigue, but also skepticism. When I joined, Teach For America was on the brink of significant expansion and reshaping. I wondered about the best way to progress the ideal of educational equity. Is it through increasing the number of corps members so that thousands more children are exposed to Teach For America teachers and fewer classrooms go unfilled? Is it through providing the best possible training and support so that retention, not mere placement, is the primary focus? Is it through focusing on the accomplishments of the alumni network, promoting the force of leaders who work to bring about change from very different arenas?

It is difficult to take the extreme position that Teach For America does absolutely no good. In the practical perspective, having Teach For America is better than the alternative of not having it. Teach For America excels at getting talented people into the classroom. Where the organization needs to improve is in its ability to give corps members the tools to succeed while they're there and in its ability to keep them in the classroom. I believe that the road ahead for Teach For America should focus not on placement, but on retention, on quality, not quantity. To some extent, Teach For America does promote inconsistency for the students, schools, and communities that need stability the most. While I don't doubt corps members' ability to become excellent teachers, too often they are excellent teachers for two short years. The quality of Teach For America is excellent, but the length of commitment isn't always enough. I believe that Teach For America can promote educational equity by focusing on effective, committed teachers who will stay in their classrooms beyond two years. I say this quite aware of the fact that I am one of the corps members who taught for just two years. I also keep in mind that Teach For America can't always influence a corps member's decision to stay or not to stay in teaching. But it can use its fund-raising ability, its network of supporters, and its national recognition to concentrate on giving corps members the tools and resources they will need to become excellent teachers for longer than two years. I continue to advocate putting more emphasis on alumni in their original placements and alumni still in education. These are the people who came to Teach For America with the purest intentions, not as a resumé builder or for the experience, but because they are career educators.

And yet the question that still nags me is whether Teach For America is a success. On a surface level, the question seems to have a straightforward answer—the thousands upon thousands of applications, the endorsements that trickle in from reputable sources, including The White House, the platitudes that boast about corps members' achievements. But there are hard realities behind the veil of Teach For America and deeper questions to pose. Can first-year teachers really make significant strides toward narrowing the achievement gap? Is Teach For America's line of preparation adequate or widely applicable? If Teach For America were to not exist, how would our most troubled schools and districts fill those teaching vacancies? And what about TFA superheroes versus TFA zeroes? Why are some corps members so successful and others mediocre? The testimonials of this book only skim the surface in answering these questions, but perhaps the lesson to learn in this line of thinking is that the desperate times in our nation's educational crisis call for desperate measures.

My Teach For America commitment ended on June 15, 2001, when I finished two years of teaching and joined the ranks of the alumni movement. The last week of school was a blur. Some students didn't show up, and those that did certainly weren't able to focus on academics. We cleaned up my classroom, stored away books and supplies, and took down bulletin boards. We made class yearbooks and reflected on how the year had gone. And of course, the last day of school was a celebration, a party with gluttonous amounts of food.

That last day brought a mix of emotions—excitement, nostalgia, and reflection. I had imagined the last day of school would be somber. I thought my students would be sad to bid me farewell. They would linger in my classroom at the final bell and express their heartfelt gratitude. I somehow envisioned myself gathering my students around me one last time, and imparting them with some kernel of sage advice before sending them off into the world.

In reality, there was a stampede when the final bell rang. Hoards of students sprinted for the door, and I stood pressed against the lockers hoping not to get trampled in the chaos. A few students waved to me as they dashed out, but there was little more than, "Bye, Ms. Ness." Within five minutes of the last bell, the hallways were empty, with only teachers peering out of their classrooms.

And so I returned to my classroom, to finish packing away my books and to complete my grades. My classroom was eerie; it was silent and lonely and bare. As I sat at my desk and glanced around the room, a wave of sadness swept over me. Things would never be the same. Teaching had forever changed me. I was not the same person that I was before the experience. My students changed me, the community where I worked changed my very essence, and I would never be graced by these children again. There would be more children in future years of teaching, but I was no longer responsible for the students of my first and second years of teaching. I felt a bit like parents must feel, when their children grow up and leave home.

As I sat there with that feeling of sadness, I could almost see my students sitting in their desks: Armando doodling on his spelling worksheet, Jessie and Fey whispering to each other while they thought I wasn't looking, James grinning at me with adorable dimples, even Jovanni slouching at his desk like it was a reclining chair. I knew that I might never see some of my students again; try as I might to keep up with them, some would move away from Oakland, some would fall out of touch. I would miss them, but I was also incredibly hopeful for them. I may never know how life turned out for each and every student—the successes they had, the mistakes they had made, the paths their lives would take. But maybe some of my students persevered through middle school, high school, and went on to college. Maybe some of my students would grow up to be parents who taught their own children the value of education. Perhaps some of my students would stay in their community and commit their lives to the betterment of children. My students were capable of all sorts of success; I can only hope that I instilled in them the confidence that they would need to succeed.

I originally thought my two years would end in triumphant glory. I thought I would be showered with accolades and laurels, congratulated and patted on the back, praised for my hard work and dedication. But really, there was no fanfare. Most teachers wished me a good summer and went their own ways.

At first I felt ignored or disappointed, but gradually I made sense of it. I admit that I wanted to feel like a hero and receive a hero's departure. But I was no hero. I was a teacher. I did my job, and I did it to the best of my ability, like so many teachers, all over the world do everyday. If there were any heroes in the situation, it was certainly my students. They survived and persevered and overcame obstacles everyday. So many people wanted to cast them aside, believed that they could not learn, and looked at them as hopeless. But my students handled life's challenges with the utmost grace and confidence. They deserved the accolades and the applause. I believed that I had come to Oakland to teach these children, but in reality, they were the ones who taught me. They taught me about courage, optimism, and the value of hard work. They taught me how to practice humility everyday. I will carry these lessons with me throughout my life, far beyond the school walls and the city of Oakland. Understanding these lessons was a satisfactory end to my Teach For America commitment. With this appreciation and admiration for my students, I turned out the lights and locked the door of Room 106 behind me.

—Molly Ness

The main obstacle we face at the end of the day is that our children have little confidence in themselves. They see the depravity and hopelessness around them . . . they inherit it. It is our job to show them an alternative. And although it is impossible for us to completely change the world around them, we can change the way that they see themselves. There is a heart that exists in every child that is resilient and hopeful. The mission of teaching is showing up every day and giving kids something to hope for.

—John Keisler (2000, New Jersey)

selected bibliography

Chaddock, Gail. "Teach For American Turns 10—and thrives." *The Christian Science Monitor*. October 26, 1999.

Clabaugh, Gary. "Teach for America." *Educational Horizons*. Spring 1992.

Clowes, George. "Teach For America Instructors Shine." *School Reform News*. September 2001.

Desai, Anand. "Innovative Preparation Key to Teach For America's Remarkable Retention Rates." In *National Council on Teacher Quality*. October 3, 2001.

Evans, Dennis. "Unqualified Teachers: A Predictable Finding." *Education Week*. October 30, 1996.

Fisher, Marc. "Pass/Fail." *The Washington Post Magazine*. April 6, 2003.

Goldstein, Andrew. "Should It Be This Easy To Become a Teacher?" *Time Magazine*. August 17, 2001.

"Good News about Public Schools in Louisiana." *National Education Association*. November 12, 2001.

Green, Loretta. "Joining the Corps: Teaching for America." *The San Jose Mercury*. October 22, 1999.

Kopp, Wendy. *One Day, All Children: The Unlikely Triumph of Teach For America and What I Learned Along the Way*. New York: Public Affairs, 2001.

Laczko-Kerr, Ildiko and David C. Berliner. Editor Gene Glass, "The Effectiveness of Teach For America and Other Under-Certified

Teachers on Student Academic Achievement: A Case of Harmful Public Policy." *Education Policy Analysis Archives.* College of Education, Arizona State Univ. September 2002.

Mintz, Susan. "America Needs Teachers, not Teach For America." *The Cavalier Daily.* October 23, 2001.

Pinksy, Josephine. "Teach For America Trying to Counteract Teacher Shortage." *The Daily Illini.* February 12, 2001.

Ross, Alec. "Touching a Million Kids." *Horizon Magazine.* November 11, 2001.

Schorr, Jonathon. "Class Action: What Clinton's National Service Program Could Learn form Teach For America." *Phi Delta Kappan.* December 1993.

Shapiro, Michael. *Who Will Teach For America?* Washington, D.C.: Farragut Publishing Company, 1993.

"Teach For America: A Viable, Valuable Source of Teachers Who Positively Affect Student Learning, Study Shows." *The Hoover Institute.* August 1, 2001.

"Teach For America's Quiet Visionary." *The Christian Science Monitor.* March 20, 2001.

"Teach For America Thrives; Detractors Begrudge Success." *Teacher Quality Bulletin.* Volume 2, Number 33. August 12, 2001.

"Teachers: low pay, low morale, high turnover." *CNN.* November 12, 2001.

Wilogren, Jodi. "Wendy Kopp, Leader of Teach For America." *The New York Times.* November 12, 2000.